W9-AWZ-000

With Oil in Their Lamps

WITH OIL IN THEIR LAMPS
FAITH, FEMINISM, AND THE FUTURE

SANDRA M. SCHNEIDERS

2000 Madeleva Lecture
in Spirituality

PAULIST PRESS
New York/Mahwah, New Jersey

Cover design by Lynn Else and Valerie L. Petro

Copyright © 2000 by Saint Mary's College, Notre Dame, Indiana

All rights reserved. No part of this book may be reproduced or transmitted in any form or by any means, electronic or mechanical, including photocopying, recording or by any information storage and retrieval system without permission in writing from the Publisher.

Library of Congress Cataloging-in-Publication Data

Schneiders, Sandra Marie.
    With oil in their lamps : faith, feminism, and the future / Sandra M. Schneiders.
        p. cm. — (Madeleva lecture in spirituality ; 2000)
        ISBN 0-8091-3966-9
        1. Feminism—Religious aspects—Catholic Church. 2. Catholic Church—Doctrines. I. Title. II. Series.
BX2347.8.W6 S27 2000
261.8´344—dc21   00-022504

Published by Paulist Press
997 Macarthur Boulevard
Mahwah, New Jersey 07430

www.paulistpress.com

Printed and bound in the
United States of America

CONTENTS

SALUTATION   1

INTRODUCTION   3

CHAPTER ONE: The Effect of Feminism
on Twentieth-Century America   7

CHAPTER TWO: The Effect of Feminism
on the Church   52

CHAPTER THREE: Looking to the Future   83

CONCLUSION   123

NOTES   126

Sandra M. Schneiders has been a member of the Sisters, Servants of the Immaculate Heart of Mary, Monroe, Michigan, since 1956. She received an M.A. in philosophy from the University of Detroit in 1967, an S.T.L. in patristics from Institut Catholique, Paris, in 1971, and an S.T.D. in scripture and spirituality from the Gregorian University, Rome, in 1975. She is currently professor of New Testament and spirituality at the Jesuit School of Theology and the Graduate Theological Union in Berkeley, California. She is the recipient of three honorary degrees and the Christian Culture Gold Medal of Assumption University in Canada, has authored six books and numerous articles, and is past president of the Society for the Study of Christian Spirituality. She has lectured throughout the United States, Canada, Taiwan, and New Zealand.

FEMINISM, AND THE FUTURE Faith, Feminism, and the Future FAITH, FEMINISM, AND THE FUTURE Faith, Feminism, and the Future FAITH, FEMINISM, AND THE FUTURE Faith, Feminism, and the Future FAITH, FEMINISM, AND THE FUTURE Faith, Feminism, and the Future FAITH, FEMINISM, AND THE FUTURE Faith, Feminism, and the Future FAITH, FEMINISM, AND THE FUTURE Faith, Feminism, and the Future FAITH, FEMINISM, AND THE FUTURE Faith, Feminism, and the Future FAITH, FEMINISM, AND THE FUTURE Faith, Feminism, and the Future FAITH, FEMINISM, AND THE FUTURE Faith, Feminism, and the Future FAITH, FEMINISM, AND THE FUTURE Faith, Feminism, and the Future FAITH, FEMINISM, AND THE FUTURE Faith, Feminism, and the Future FAITH, FEMINISM, AND THE FUTURE Faith, Feminism, and the Future FAITH, FEMINISM, AND THE FUTURE Faith, Feminism, and the Future FAITH, FEMINISM, AND THE FUTURE Faith, Feminism, and the Future FAITH, FEMINISM, AND THE FUTURE Faith, Feminism, and the Future FAITH, FEMINISM, AND THE FUTURE Faith, Feminism, and the Future FAITH, FEMINISM, AND THE FUTURE Faith, Feminism, and the Future FAITH, FEMINISM, AND THE

To my friend

Kathleen O'Brien, I.H.M.,

whose lamp is never empty

WITH OIL IN THEIR LAMPS
FAITH, FEMINISM, AND THE FUTURE

SALUTATION

President Eldred, members of the board of trustees, distinguished faculty, students, fellow Madeleva lecturers, and honored guests, it is a distinct privilege to have been asked to deliver the millennial Madeleva Lecture in Spirituality at Saint Mary's College, which became my honorary alma mater in 1998. It is a special joy to participate in this event with the scholars, all of whom are here tonight, who, over the past fifteen years, have shared the honor and the responsibility of delivering these Madeleva Lectures. My indebtedness to the great woman for whom this lectureship is named, Sister Mary Madeleva Wolff, president of this college for twenty-seven years, will be evident in all that follows.[1] Madeleva was a Religious of the Congregation of the Holy Cross, a creative and demanding educator of women, and a protofeminist who would not have applied that word to herself or perhaps even recognized it, but who was coloring outside the patriarchal lines long before we realized that those lines did not, in fact, provide the whole picture. Madeleva was also a first-class

1

scholar and a renowned poet who is no doubt very much enjoying the fact that her memory is being celebrated not by a fancy tea or even a fund-raiser, although she enjoyed the first and was remarkably good at the second, but by an exchange of ideas on matters of religious, intellectual, and cultural substance. I am proud to be part of celebrating her memory.

INTRODUCTION

Naming the century that slipped into the past a few months ago will provide material for conversation for some time to come. Was it the century of world wars or of worldwide struggle for liberation? Was it the nuclear century, in which we finally became capable of definitively reversing creation by destroying ourselves and our planet, or the ecological century, when we finally committed ourselves to not doing so? Was its major turning point the industrial revolution or the technological revolution, that is, the machine or the computer? Did space travel, which offered us the first outside glimpse of our tiny, blue-green planet, or earth travel, which brought us face-to-face with our multicolored and multicultured neighbors in the global village, define the twentieth century? Was it medical advances, which doubled our biological life expectancy, or the information sciences, which multiplied exponentially our ability to communicate, that really shaped the century? Or was it perhaps a century best defined by its succession of "generations": immigrants, flappers, survivors of the Great Depression, the suburbanites and the Waltons, the baby boomers, the '60s radicals, the me-generation, or generation X?

I am going to suggest that the culminating contribution of the second millennium, the defining characteristic of the twentieth century, and the most important source of energy for the immediate future is the emergence of women, the beginning of the recognition of the full personhood of half the human family. This revolution affects all races, nations, ethnic groups, religions, and social classes not just from without but from within. The twentieth century will, I believe, finally be recognized as the "century of women." In what follows I want to look at the emergence in and effects of feminism on American culture, and how feminism, largely through the mediation of women's Religious Life and especially its promotion of the higher education of women, has affected the Church. I will then look at what the Church, specifically through the example of Jesus as he is presented in the Gospel, can contribute to the transformation of cultural feminism into a prophetic force moving all creation toward a future in God's universal *shalom*. Finally, I will raise the question of how women Religious, who once carried out almost alone the task of educating Catholic women, can effectively join in equal and mutually enriching partnership with other women and men to carry forward into a new cultural and ecclesial situation the project of preparing

4

Christian women for the Gospel work of liberation and justice, now understood within a feminist context. In a way, I am asking what Sister Madeleva would be doing if she were among us today.

CHAPTER ONE
THE EFFECT OF FEMINISM ON TWENTIETH-CENTURY AMERICA

Feminism is a worldwide movement that has taken many forms and means different things to different people. I will define it, for purposes of this essay, as a comprehensive ideology, rooted in women's experience of sexually-based oppression, that engages in a critique of patriarchy as an essentially dysfunctional system, embraces an alternative vision for humanity and the earth, and actively seeks to bring this vision to realization. Without pausing to elaborate at length on each member of this definition, which I have done elsewhere,[2] I would highlight the following important features of feminism so defined. First, feminism is not merely a cause or a project but a comprehensive ideology, that is, a mentality or life stance that colors all of one's commitments and activities. Second, although feminism is concerned with the full humanity of all people, it is rooted in women's experience of oppression, just as Latin American liberation theology is based in the experience of the poor and Black

7

liberation in the experience of people of color. Third, it is not purely theoretical or exclusively reactive, but embraces analysis, a vision of a different reality, and an active participation in change to bring about that different reality.

Contemporary feminism's roots are in the long history of *women's movements* that, in this country, came to fruition for the first time in 1920, when women achieved the right to vote by virtue of the Nineteenth Amendment to the Constitution. A "second wave" of the movement for the *emancipation* of women developed in the 1960s as women participating in the Civil Rights struggle saw the connection between racial oppression and gender oppression. This second wave developed into a "third wave" or what has become known as the *women's liberation movement*. This movement is concerned not simply with the social, political, and economic equality of women with men but with a fundamental re-imagination of the whole of humanity in relation to the whole of reality, including nonhuman creation. In other words, as feminist consciousness has gradually deepened, the feminist agenda has widened, from a concern to right a particular structural wrong, namely, the exclusion of women from the voting booth, to a demand for full participation of women in society and culture, to an ideal of recreating humanity itself according to a pattern of ecojustice, that is, of right relations at every level and in relation to all of reality. In this first chapter I want to talk about how structural changes have affected the status of women and how the resulting changes in the cultural imagination have begun to effect the redefinition of humanity.

A. PROGRESS TOWARD EQUALITY THROUGH STRUCTURAL CHANGE

No matter how a person evaluates the situation, there is no disputing the fact that the status of women in this country has changed dramatically since 1920 and seismically since 1960. Nor, whether one approves of it or not, can there be any dispute about the direction of the change. It has been toward equality of women with men. And finally, it is clear that most basic to this change of status has been the gradual modification of the social structures that enshrined, expressed, maintained, and enforced women's inferior status. Women's full equality in family and society is still a long way off, but it is no longer an issue that can be trivialized. I will discuss the structural changes that have affected women's status under three headings: movement toward self-possession, movement toward agency, and movement toward self-determination.

1. The Movement toward Self-possession

The basis of women's oppression is gender. Simply being a woman has, historically, meant being not a full person but an inferior and derivative version of the human. In this construction of reality, the male, by virtue of being male, is superior and by natural right the superior owns and controls the inferior. Because the imputed inferiority of women is rooted specifically in their femaleness, the primary locus of male control has always been women's sexuality. Very basic to the movement for women's liberation, both symbolically and politically, has been women's effort to "take back their sexuality," to undermine the male claim to ownership and reestablish the personal right of women to sexual self-possession.

Although women in our society continue to suffer massive oppression in the area of sexuality, the progress that has been made in just a few decades, if viewed against the background of millennia of male domination, is startling in its depth and extent. The myriad forms of sexual abuse of women, which were not even considered abuse until very recently, are now recognized as such and even criminalized. Rape is no longer seen as "merely" the result of uncontrollable sexual passion but as a violent crime. Incest and pedophilia as well as marital rape, all of which have been accepted from time immemorial as the prerogative of the male head of household, have been criminalized. Acquaintance or date rape is no longer qualitatively distinguished from stranger rape, and neither can be defended in a court of law by claiming that the victim was "asking for it" or "really didn't object even though she said 'no.' " Most recently public outrage has been turned on the punitive rape of women in war and the sexual violation of women in prison by male institutional personnel. When we consider that until very recently, of all these forms of sexual abuse of women, only the most flagrant form of violent stranger rape was considered criminal, and even that crime was difficult to prosecute because the victim was usually considered responsible in some way for her violation, the present situation, in terms of social structures, is remarkable. The revisions of law, arrests, prosecutions, sentencing, and postsentence follow-up of sexual offenders reflects the very new conviction that women are by natural right as sexually inviolate as men always have been. Their sexuality is intrinsic to their personhood, and no man has a right to invade it, possess it, control it, or use it for his purposes. He may legitimately enter the sphere of a woman's sexuality only at her free invitation and on her terms. Sexual inviolability is the symbol of personal self-possession.

At an even deeper level, public consciousness is gradually coming to accept that sexual intimidation, even if no act of physical violence occurs, is also a crime against the person of a woman. Intimidation on the street and in the workplace now has a name, harassment, and a status, illegal. Furthermore, even if no epithets are hurled or suggestive actions performed, the man who uses sex to intimidate through denial of promotion or other benefits can now be charged and prosecuted for discrimination. In short, women as a class are increasingly recognized as having rights to immunity from sexual exploitation for male profit or discrimination on the basis of gender.

My purpose in retailing these widely acknowledged facts is to point out that what has happened in the short span of approximately three decades is revolutionary. Although the physical, psychological, and economic abuse of women through their sexuality is far from being a thing of the past, the recognition— at least among intelligent and fair-minded people, especially among women themselves— of the full and equal personhood of women has been accomplished. Women have moved from being the possessions of men to self-possession as persons.

2. The Movement toward Personal Agency

Self-possession, personhood, implies agency, the ability to act from one's own center for one's own purposes rather than living in complete dependence on the will of another and in service to his purposes. Women's long history of dependence on men for their very livelihood expressed in the depletion of their life's force in producing and raising men's children and serving as a support system for men's projects has, again in a very short span of time, been subverted by a change in social, economic, and political structures and especially through education. The struggle of women for equality in the workplace is hydra-headed and far from over. Virginia Woolf claimed that what a woman needed for full agency was a room of her own, that is, a physical and psychic sphere in which she was not totally consumed by the needs of others, and an income sufficient to sustain herself and over which she had some control.[3]

The quest for the symbolic coins of autonomy has been the focus of women's struggle in the *economic* arena. The flagship issue of equal pay for equal work, as most people realize whether or not they support the agenda, is a Trojan horse in the walled city of patriarchy. Hidden within it are such issues as what work is important in society, what makes it important, and how the world of work should be structured. Women claiming equality in the workplace are demanding not just an equitable paycheck but a complete re-visioning of the world of work and, by implication, of the family as the basic unit of society.

If women are to be treated equally in the workplace both economically and personally, they can no longer bear the entire burden of child-raising and home maintenance. Not only must fathers accept equal responsibility for their children, but affordable child care and safe schools become an urgent necessity. Furthermore, women's unique and protracted role in reproduction has to become as definitive of the structure of the workplace as male freedom from such responsibility has been in the past. Artificial barriers to work in fields previously seen as part of the "man's world" such as construction, electrical and plumbing jobs, professorships, law, long-distance driving, medicine, ministry, entrepreneurship, leadership of major companies, police and fire prevention work, and so on must come down. Women cannot be restricted to teaching small children, social work, nursing, and secretarial positions, and if they freely choose such fields of endeavor, they deserve to be paid in terms of the value of the work itself, which, in turn, changes the criterion of important work from who does it to what is being done. Once women are established in fields formerly reserved to men and have effectively demanded the pay and the status their work deserves, they are in a position to change the way business is carried on, whether the business is education or technology, medicine or politics.

Women still struggle with such issues as being denied credit independent of marital status, being penalized by inheritance laws, and being demeaned and patronized in their attempts to establish ownership of real estate or automobiles. They are still often denied quality service from hotels, restaurants, banks, airlines, and service providers and still often receive inferior health care. But women who refuse to accept this implied economic dependence are, individually and collectively, taking the offenders to court for redress of grievances, and they are beginning to win.

Equality in the economic sphere may be the last bastion of patriarchal resistance in secular society because of the connection in the capitalist system between money and power. But there is little doubt that the right of men to determine how women will and will not participate in the economic sphere has been definitively undermined. Like the Berlin Wall, this ultimate defense of male power will come down of its own weight when the symbolic one hundredth monkey pounces upon it. And that monkey is poised to spring.

The move toward agency has been most evident, in a sense, in the political sphere. Women's right to vote, like freedom from slavery for African Americans, required an amendment to the U.S. Constitution, which is not only extremely difficult to achieve politically but is highly symbolic of the fact that a genuinely new situation has emerged in this country. Amending the Constitution is an acknowledgment that something that was not and could not have been foreseen at the founding of the nation, but was nevertheless implicit in its founding principles, has emerged as so important for society that the nation cannot proceed without explicitly recognizing it. The right to vote in a democracy is symbolic of political personhood and is in reality the basic form of political agency.

Although it has taken decades for women to realize the leverage they could collectively exercise through the vote, they have begun to unite across lines of party, class, race, and religion, as no other group of voters does or can, on issues of special importance to women as women, such as women's health, reproductive rights, children's rights, economic equity, and freedom from sexual violence and discrimination. No politician today can afford to alienate the women's vote, and no candidate will be elected without the support of a significant proportion of the women in this country. Women are still achieving their political ends primarily by electing men who will represent their interests but, as the number of women in both houses of Congress, on the bench of the Supreme Court, in governors' mansions, and mayors' offices increases and the election of a woman as president becomes more conceivable every four years, women are moving steadily toward equal participation in the government of the country. And it is already evident that women with political power not only have some different items on their agenda from men but also have some very different perspectives on a number of issues.

The third sphere in which women's agency has become increasingly evident is that of education. Since 1918 every state in the nation has mandated universal education for both boys and girls up to the age of at least fourteen, and usually sixteen.[4] But, as professional educators have been insisting for years, the education of boys and girls has not been equal.[5] Schools have been organized to promote the educational future of male children, with an operative assumption that girls did not need and probably would not pursue higher education. In the classroom, boys demand and receive a disproportionate amount of teachers' energy and attention.[6] Boys' contributions are given priority. Boys are encouraged to succeed in mathematics, the hard sciences, and technology, that is, in those fields that will be economically profitable in the future. Conversely, girls are discouraged, by subtle social pressure as well as low expectations and lack of mentoring, from excelling in any field but especially in those implicitly reserved to boys.[7] The educational experience from the earliest years is agonistic and competitive, discouraging and disparaging female ways of learning and modes of knowing.[8]

But this picture is also changing as feminist consciousness has been brought to bear on the educational system. In a comparatively brief span of time, historically speaking, women have begun to level the playing field of the academy. Two factors have contributed to this phenomenon: First, the development of women's schools and colleges (a topic to which we will return), which has fostered women's educational initiative and valorized their approaches to learning while providing role models and an expectation of academic excellence. Second, the insistence that women be admitted as equals to once all-male schools and colleges has broken down the separate and unequal approach to the education of males and females. The ratio of women to men graduating from high school, going to college, completing professional degrees in medicine and law, and earning doctoral degrees in both the sciences and the humanities has changed dramatically, with women now equaling or outnumbering men in some areas.[9] Women are still far behind men in obtaining faculty positions in higher education, and the system is still organized to prevent qualified women from being promoted or receiving tenure.[10] On average, women professors still receive lower salaries than their equally qualified (and sometimes less productive) male colleagues, and far fewer women hold presidencies at major universities. Research money is still disproportionately directed to men, whose capabilities are often deemed superior to women's and whose projects are still often considered more serious and substantive.

Nevertheless, the handwriting is on the wall in the academy, as it is in the economic and political spheres. Discrimination in hiring, promotion, and salaries is increasingly publicized and protested, and redress is increasingly obtained. Anti-harassment policies are making women students less vulnerable to sexual bullying for grades or mentoring, while inclusive-language policies are protecting them from belittling and abuse in the classroom. Institutions of higher education know that they have to progress quickly toward gender parity in hiring, if for no other reason than the desire to attract women students who no longer want to spend their entire educational careers listening exclusively to men talking about men. Women's studies programs and even departments, which were objects of mild ridicule twenty years ago, are now taken very seriously at major universities, and their graduates are eagerly sought to staff similar programs arising elsewhere. And few courses are considered even adequate today if they take no account of the feminist critique of the field, include no women authors in their bibliographies, and make no attempt to include feminist methodology in their procedures.

In short, in the economic, political, and educational spheres, women are both changing institutions and structures in their favor and using the resources they thereby acquire to bring about further change. In all of these areas women are moving from nearly total dependence on men toward increasing personal agency.

3. The Movement toward Self-determination

The ultimate expression of agency is self-determination, the active assumption of the right and the power to decide who one will be and how one will function in the world and thus exert significant influence on history and culture. As long as women were the possession of men and virtually totally dependent upon men, it was men who decided who women were, what they were capable of, where and how they were to function, and for what ends. In general, women were to produce and raise men's descendants and serve as support systems for the men who were engaged in the historical task of cultural creation. As women have begun to throw off the sexual subordination that made them property and to achieve economic, political, and educational leverage, they have begun to effect a personal revolution that has enormous consequences. But in this area the situation is extremely ambiguous.

First, women have become increasingly autonomous in the *sexual* sphere. To a significant degree, first-world women have succeeded in withdrawing their sexuality and reproductive power from male control, which has brought about a revolution in regard to society's basic unit, the family. As both contraception and abortion as well as divorce that is relatively free of social stigma have become widely and legally available, women have been empowered to decide for themselves how they will relate to the issues of extramarital sex, marriage, and parenthood.

Antifeminists, both male and female, have been quick to point out the social dislocation that women's sexual emancipation has precipitated. The political code words "family values" thinly disguises the dominative agenda of reestablishing patriarchy in society, beginning in the home and the school. The implied argument that the patriarchal system served us well in a mythical golden age of domestic order is both false and cynical. At the surface level it served men well by freeing them from onerous relational responsibilities and supplying them with an unpaid support system. However, at a deeper level it was also dysfunctional for men since it deprived society of women's contributions and men of the impetus to personal development that mutuality in relationships and participation in childrearing might have offered. But the unanswered question at this point is: What is the alternative? Certainly familial good order bought at the price of women's personhood, agency, and self-determination is too expensive. But women's replication of traditional male narcissism and irresponsibility resulting in social instability, violence, and neglect of children is hardly a desirable version of equality.

Women's increasing participation in the *economic* system is also ambiguous in some respects. On the one hand, women with the capacity to support themselves are free to marry if and when they choose rather than being passed from father to husband as dependent property. But on the other hand, women are much less free, for both financial and social reasons, to choose to remain at home to raise their children even during the first weeks and months of a child's life. Even an intact marriage usually requires two salaries, and divorce most often leaves the woman with responsibility to raise the children, often without financial or psychological support from the father.[11] Women working full-time outside the home still carry a disproportionate share of the homemaking and child-rearing responsibilities, which keeps many women from making progress in their careers comparable to that of men who do not have or do not accept such responsibilities. Thus women, especially if they are divorced and/or are single parents, have higher costs and fewer assets with which to handle them. And, to aggravate the situation, the more responsible they are to their families the less likely they are to advance occupationally and therefore economically. Again, the answer cannot be returning women to the status of indentured servants, but it is not clear how women's economic agency can be exercised to their own advantage without replicating the very attitudes and behaviors, especially toward children, that feminists have deplored in the patriarchal system.

In summary, the remarkable developments during the second half of the twentieth century in societal attitudes and structures in the areas of sexuality, economics, politics, and education have effected a profound change in the status of women. Although many women, especially poor and minority women, still do not participate equitably in these changes, women as a group have moved steadily toward self-possession, personal agency, and self-determination, understood to a large extent as increasing equality with men in society. It should come as no surprise that this development has raised, in a new way, the question of morality. With freedom comes responsibility. But freedom is never absolute and the social context in which women have become, at least to some extent, historical subjects rather than patriarchal objects is structured almost exclusively by the liberal version of patriarchal values: individualism, unrestrained greed, materialism, ruthless competition, and violence. To participate on an equal footing in such a system does not seem to allow for the realization of the alternative vision of reality that the third wave of feminism projects.

B. Progress toward a Redefinition of Humanity through Imaginative Change

At this point I want to change the focus of this analysis to explore what may be ultimately more important than the structural changes in regard to gender and the resulting changes in behavior, namely the revolution in the imagination that these changes have helped to effect. An imaginative change is not simply a modification of ideas or policies. It is a new world construction, a different, affectively loaded, wholistic vision of reality.

Imagination, as I am using it here, is not a producer of fantasy or even of a dream of what might be. It is a "take" on what presently is, the dynamic picture of reality within which we function without realizing that we are part of that picture, much less that there might be something wrong with that picture. The patriarchal imagination that controlled all experience, that of women as well as men, for centuries was a way of "seeing," a grid through which everything was perceived and experienced. The patriarchal grid, which was itself invisible, arranged all of reality in terms of male-dominative relationships, justified the resulting attitudes and behaviors of domination and subordination, assigned status, power, and privilege in society accordingly, and created the overwhelming sense that this was not a human arrangement, much less a sinful one, but simply the way things naturally, and even by divine decree, are meant to be.

The patriarchal imagination is, above all, a grid for the understanding of humanity within which the human race is hierarchically divided according to various dualistic principles, yielding pairs in which one member of each pair is superior and the other inferior. Thus, humanity consists of whites and people of color, masters and slaves, adults and children, rich and poor, clergy and laity, royalty and commoners, and so on. But basic to all of these dualisms is the fundamental, biologically based, ontologically unchangeable, paradigmatic dualism: male-female. In each of the pairs one member is "masculine," that is, autonomous and self-determining, endowed with power and agency that are exercised upon the "feminine" member, which is owned and other-determined, powerless and dependent.

Imaginative changes are not usually effected by the presentation of ideas or by logical arguments any more than the imagination of the world as a flat surface or the center of the universe yielded to scientific proof that neither is true. Indeed, because the imagination provides a reality construction and therefore the context for all experience, people usually vigorously resist any revision of the master images of God, world, and self that hold reality together in ordinary experience. The ecclesiastical resistance to Galileo makes little sense at the level of a theoretical discussion about scientific ideas but very good sense when his discoveries are seen as an assault on the world image that structured medieval life.

Imaginative changes are brought about by shock, experiences that unsettle the whole picture of reality and require that we reconstruct our universe in some new way. The story of Oscar Romero, the timid ecclesiastic who became the fearless champion of the Salvadoran poor, or that of Catherine of Siena, the reclusive contemplative who became one of the major agents of social change in fourteenth-century Italy, illustrates how imaginative change occurs. When Romero saw, in the flesh of his tortured and martyred priest-friend, Rutilio Grande, how the social system in which he believed actually operated, he did not simply change his political ideas; his world changed. When Catherine experienced in prayer the Jesus of her intimate religious experience outside the door of her cell telling her to come out of her solitude into ministry, her self-understanding underwent a revolution, and for the next thirteen years she labored tirelessly in the social and political-ecclesiastical arenas. One can, of course, resist imaginative shock and simply refuse to engage the new reality. Often this resistance takes the form of violence against the catalyst, as was the case in the Church's persecution of Galileo. But for those like Romero and Catherine, who engage the newness, the change in behavior may be sudden or it may take place gradually as the implications of the new vision reveal themselves. The important point is that we are talking not primarily about a change of ideas or of policies but about a change of worldview. It is this changed perception of the whole that leads to changed ideas, revised behaviors, and even the restructuring of institutions.

In the past few decades, at least in the first world (and increasingly elsewhere), the patriarchal imagination has received a series of profound shocks that have polarized society into those who have begun to engage the emerging reality of women's full personhood and those who have committed themselves to resisting any revision of the patriarchal status quo. I want to talk about two of these shocks, one in the world of popular culture and one in the world of education.

1. Women's Emergence in the World of Athletics

I think that in this country one of the most effective shocks to the patriarchal imagination has occurred in the realm of athletics or sports. History may prove that the passage of Title IX, which decreed that women must have the same access to athletics as men in institutions, such as schools, receiving federal funds, was as important as the Nineteenth Amendment or *Roe v. Wade* in restructuring the sexual imagination in this country.[12] Whether or not that conjecture is verified, it is already clear that the emergence of women as major participants in the sphere of athletics, both amateur and professional, has been a significant factor in the reimagining of women's reality and of the relationship between the sexes.

Sports plays an enormously important role in American culture, both symbolically and economically.[13] Any in-depth psycho-sociological analysis of this complex phenomenon is well beyond the scope of this essay. However, it takes no special psychoanalytic insight to recognize that the rugged individualism, pioneering self-confidence, competitiveness, expansionism, and messianic sense of destiny with the implied right to conquer, dominate, dispossess, and banish are well summed up in the triumphant shout of the American athlete, "I am number one!"

American athletes, both arrogantly and somewhat ludicrously, do not even restrict their claims to their own country. Sports played seriously only in this country culminate in "world" championships. There is little doubt that the national liturgy is the Super Bowl, the "world championship" of American football, when not only a trophy and a title are awarded to the winning team but, significantly, a ring, the ancient symbol of the academic doctorate, episcopal ordination, and accession to the royal throne, is conferred on each of the individual players. The choice of the Most Valuable Player assures that no team ethos will submerge the individual. Every player competes not just with the opposing team but with his own team-mates, because until he has vanquished absolutely everyone, friend as well as foe, and stands in solitary splendor as sole victor, he has not really achieved his goal.

The exorbitant (if not obscene, in view of the destitution of millions in this country and abroad) salaries paid to professional athletes in this country underline the symbolic role of athletics. I would suggest that the primary symbolism of sports among Americans lies in its definition of humanity. The ideal of the American psyche is not the saint, the scholar, the humanitarian, the diplomat, or the artist. It is the consummate athlete. We try, subconsciously perhaps, but very really to deny the evident baseness of this ideal by talking about the mental and psychological aspects of athletic competition, the character-building potential of team play and good sportsmanship, the constructive release of aggression, and even the moral demand that athletic heroes be role models for young Americans. But, in fact, the American definition of the paragon of humanity is a physically powerful male who is willing and able to pulverize, physically or symbolically, any and all competition.

The world of athletics, even more than that of economics or politics, has been a "man's world." It was the one arena in which men felt that they would never be challenged by women because it was defined by physical superiority to which men seemed to have a biologically ineradicable claim. But, taking no chances, they made sure that girls and women were discouraged from mounting any challenge by making their participation in sports economically nonfeasible and socially unacceptable.

Title IX, however, was the beginning of the end of male dominance in the world of sports. By the time girls had had a decade of mandated equal access to the resources necessary for athletic development, women athletes had begun to close the gap between themselves and males in many areas. No longer was there only the occasional lone exception that proved the rule: the preadolescent gymnast, surreal ice dancer, the Wimbledon tennis champion, or the preternaturally talented female golfer. Women were turning in spectacular performances in every event of field and track, which has defined classic athletics since the days of Greece and Rome. They were swimming every event men had with extraordinary strength, grace, and speed. They were organizing baseball, basketball, volleyball, and soccer teams and creating leagues in which to play them. Women were no longer jogging breathlessly over five kilometer routes while the men ran marathons. They were running the same marathons and completing the same iron-man triple-event challenges as the men, rapidly closing not only the gaps in endurance, strength, and skill, but even in speed.

Two events symbolically, economically, and socially shocked the American imagination in the realm of women's sports: the 1988 Summer Olympics, in which the U.S. women's team brought home the majority of the medals while the men turned in a lackluster performance and during which the spectacular all-around athlete, Florence Griffith Joyner,[14] emerged as probably the best athlete, male or female, in the world; and the world soccer championship played in 1999 between China and the U.S. before ninety thousand fans in the bleachers, including the president of the United States, and hundreds of thousands more all over the world via television. Although women athletes in general still lag far behind men in financial rewards, even that gap is beginning to close.

I am dwelling on this development in women's athletics because of its significance for the American definition of ideal humanity. If athletics supplies the norm for human excellence and women can perform athletically as well as men, which is becoming increasingly clear, then humanity can no longer be defined, ideally, as the powerful male. We may continue to define it as the superb athlete but that ideal now comes in two sexes. Few men can play 120 minutes of soccer at breakneck speed, run the mile in minutes, swim or dive with Olympic perfection. The women who do these things are not aberrations of nature but women at their physical best. And women at their physical best are every bit as impressive as men at theirs. It is no longer the case that men are the only paragons and that some men are what all men but no women potentially are. Some men and some women are what all men and women, supposedly, aspire to be. Just as women saints and scholars have made continued male supremacy in the Church and academy possible only by enforced discrimination, so male supremacy in the physical realm is no longer based on any biological or ontological claim. To achieve the ideal is to subvert the exclusivist claim at its foundation. I think a sign that this imaginative transformation is taking place is the increasing occurrence of coed sports. Boys and girls in grade school and even, in some cases, in high school can be seen playing on the same teams, a proleptic symbol of a new world.

But the phenomenon of women's accession to athletic prominence is not a one-way dynamic. Not only have women been changed by access to athletics but women are changing the understanding of sports. Brute force is gradually being, if not demythologized, at least relativized by the equally attractive ideals of endurance, grace, beauty, strength, and precision. Women's relational approach to both individual and team sports is raising questions about whether competition has to be about ruthlessness, destructive violence, and the humiliation if not obliteration of the opponent. Is war, which makes the opponent an enemy, the only metaphor for sports, or might not the friendly game between mutually respectful competitors be a metaphor more conducive to civilized entertainment among humans?

31

The evident relishing by so many Americans of the fact that the women Olympians and soccer champions are real people who hold real jobs in the real world and play sports for fun as well as fame, who do not rely for strength or skill on alcohol or drugs but on training and practice, who promote their teammates and befriend their opponents while relishing learning about other cultures and peoples, and who do not batter (or even murder) their spouses or children, choke their coaches or spit on the officials or fight other players, or engage in "entitlement" sexual abuse and promiscuity suggests that the influence of women athletes may extend well beyond the playing field. These women are role models for boys as well as girls, for men as well as women.

However, the ambiguity noted above regarding the advances of women through changes in economic, political, and educational structures is also evident in the athletic realm. Women do not come to athletics as an ideal sphere of human endeavor that they can shape to their own desires. Sports is a world structured from time immemorial by men. It is heavily burdened by the idealization of violence on and off the field, obscene greed, childish narcissism, cutthroat competitiveness, and shady business practice. Even the Olympic games, that monument to the highest ideals of sports and sportsmanship, have been besmirched by dishonesty and corrupt politics, and tainted by nationalistic violence.

Women entering the upper echelons of the world of sports can easily see equality in this field, as in others, in terms of sameness, of duplicating male experience that is regarded as normative. What does it mean when women want to become boxers, to participate in a so-called sport whose avowed end is to render another human being unconscious, regardless of the fact that this sometimes leads to death and usually to long-term impairment? What does it mean that some women want to play football, another sport devoted to damaging physical attack on others? Is the only way for women to become full participants in the world of sports to espouse the violence and destructiveness that have made male athletics such a bloody business? It may well be the case that women's athletic coming-of-age, which has shocked the patriarchal imagination into a recognition of women's participation in the ideal of humanity, will help deal the final blow to the teetering wall of sexual apartheid in American culture. But whether women athletes will transform professional sports or sports will dehumanize women is a topic on which the jury is still out.

2. Women's Participation in Higher Education

A second shock to the patriarchal imagination of first-world culture has been occasioned by the entrance of women into the realms of higher education. This shock has affected our conception not only of humanity but of knowledge itself, and a shift in our conception of knowledge is a shift in our "take" on reality as a whole. The entrance of women, and with them the feminist agenda, into the academy has affected the fields of literature, history, art and music, anthropology, sociology and psychology, and perhaps to a lesser extent the hard sciences. But given the context of the Madeleva Lectures and my agenda in the next part of the essay of analyzing the effect of feminism on the Church, I will concentrate on the field of theology.

Prior to 1943, when Sister Madeleva Wolff inaugurated the graduate School of Sacred Theology for the preparation of teachers of religion in Catholic schools, Catholic women were not allowed to study theology.[15] Today, not sixty years later, women are still excluded from ordained ministry in the Catholic Church but have equaled or outnumbered men students in graduate programs in theology.[16]

The active presence of women as full members and as officers in the Catholic Theological Society of America, the Catholic Biblical Association, the Canon Law Society of America, the College Theology Society, the American Academy of Religion, and the Society of Biblical Literature has steadily increased, and the literary output of women theologians has become notable in quantity and quality.[17] The Madeleva Lectures themselves, over the past fifteen years, have provided contributions in the areas of ecclesiology, ministry, biblical studies, liturgy, history of spirituality, systematic theology, religious education, practical theology, and ministry.[18] The recently established Distinguished Catholic Women Theologians Lectureship at Boston College is further recognition that women are no longer an exception or a curiosity but an important and distinctive voice in the professional theological conversation.

I would like to single out two types of contribution, reciprocally influencing each other, that feminist theological scholarship (whether coming from women or from men) has made or fostered: the first is a substantive modification of theological content and method; the second is a challenge to the overall approach to theological scholarship.

a. Theological Content and Method

While it is not possible to even list, much less summarize, the major contributions of feminist scholars in the various subdisciplines of theology, it is instructive to mention a few major shifts that these contributions have occasioned or fostered. Elisabeth Schüssler Fiorenza's groundbreaking book, *In Memory of Her*, systematically reinterpreted every book of the New Testament through the lens of a feminist hermeneutics of suspicion and retrieval with the avowed purpose of restoring women to Christian history and their religious history to Christian women. It was a major effort to deal with the destructive effect on women of the patriarchal bias of the biblical text and the launching of a full-scale agenda of contemporary feminist biblical interpretation.[19] The originality of this agenda in relation to earlier efforts was that its purpose was no longer to rescue the biblical text from those accusing it of bias or error, but to rescue women victimized by the text itself as well as by the history of its interpretation from the legitimation of their oppression by appeal to the Word of God. Furthermore, the agenda has broadened and deepened from reinterpreting the text itself from a feminist perspective and for feminist purposes to calling into question the basic hermeneutical theory that has legitimated and even necessitated oppressive interpretation and use of the text. This, in turn, has led to a questioning of the patriarchal processes that originally limited the canon itself by excluding first- and second-century texts that accorded a larger or more favorable role to women in early Christianity. The development of feminist biblical interpretation is far from complete. And whether scholars are elated or distressed by the development, it is no longer possible to do biblical business as usual. Feminist hermeneutics has moved from the periphery to the center of biblical scholarship.

In the area of systematic theology the three major topics of feminist revision have been the theology of God, the theology of Christ, and the theology of Church. Two significant works on the Trinity by Catholic feminist scholars appeared within a year of each other: Catherine LaCugna's *God for Us* in 1991 and Elizabeth A. Johnson's *She Who Is* in 1992.[20] Dealing with the ascribed masculinity of God in all three "persons" was a radical subversion of theological androcentrism and patriarchy with implications for the pervasive sexism of the Church as institution. The work of feminist theologians on the question of God administered repeated shocks to the religious and the theological imagination. It forced people, including professional theologians, to acknowledge that their God-image was a human construction rather than divine revelation. Once again, the feminist re-visioning was not limited to a questioning of substance but pushed the questions of theological presuppositions and methodology, hermeneutics of texts, interaction of theological theory with liturgical practice and spirituality, and how tendential theology affects the religious psyche.

Christology has also felt the impact of feminist theological scholarship. Beginning with Rosemary Radford Ruether's famous article, "Can a Male Saviour Save Women?" [21] feminist theologians have struggled with the significance of the biological maleness of Jesus for women (and men) believers. Here especially, the pastoral significance of a theological question became painfully evident as the Vatican appealed to Jesus' sex as the basis for the exclusion of women from ordained ministry. [22] This patriarchal agenda of the official Church has tended to control the feminist discussion of Christology among Catholic scholars, but Christology has also been the front on which feminism has had some of its most enlightening encounters with the transformative agendas of other movements such as liberation theology, Black theology, Asian theology, missiology, ecumenism, and interreligious dialogue.[23] Basic to the reexamination of how we understand Jesus of Nazareth as the Christ is the issue of particularity in God's work of universal salvation. The struggle is joined at the level of exclusionary and dominative understandings of particularity versus inclusive and egalitarian understandings of universality.[24] The maleness of the earthly Jesus is an aspect of his particularity even as his messianic identity is the basis of his role in universal salvation. Feminist theology is not the only influence in the transformation of the christological agenda, but it has played a highly significant role in bringing a new set of issues into the center of theological work.

Ecclesiology and liturgy have been, perhaps, the most neuralgic areas of theological engagement for feminists in general and theologians in particular. The Church has been, almost from the beginning, a patriarchal institution. Within a few decades of its foundation in Easter faith, male Christians began to assume ownership and directorship of the institution and to restrict ever more stringently the role of women believers within it. Women were rapidly banished from liturgical roles as the gates to ordained ministry clanged shut behind them and the flaming sword of sexism was stationed at the threshold. Today, women like Joan Chittister,[25] Denise Carmody,[26] and Mary Collins,[27] who are trying to open the institutional Church and its ministry to the vocations and gifts of women, are pushing a sisyphean boulder of nearly eighteen hundred years' weight up the greased hill of a fiercely defended male power structure.

Although visible gains have been relatively slight so far, the sheer intensity of male resistance to women's claim to equality in the Church has precipitated a remarkable output of scholarship in the field of ecclesiology by both women and men who have returned again and again to the issues of Church foundation and the will of Jesus for the Church, authority in the Church, ministry and sexuality, baptismal equality within the People of God, the universality of the call to mission and ministry, liturgical leadership, sacramental theory and practice, dissent in the Church, infallibility, the role of theology in the formation of the *sensus fidelium* and of the *sensus fidelium* in the development of doctrine, the relation of the local to the universal Church, and so on. Almost every question on the contemporary theological agenda has ramifications in the area of ecclesiology, and the social practice of being Church influences every area of discussion. Women have not been alone in raising the burning questions in the area of ecclesiology, but the feminist analysis and agenda have been a major catalyst for this discussion, which was central to the work of Vatican II and has been on the front burner ever since: What is the Church, what is it called to be and do, and how can it respond to that calling in a modern (and now postmodern) global context?

Without wishing to slight other important areas of discussion influenced by women's participation in the theological enterprise of the Church, I will end this brief survey by indicating the role of feminist theologians such as Lisa Sowle Cahill[28] and Margaret Farley[29] in the sphere of moral theology. One might say that the experience of women, especially in the area of sexuality, has been the unacknowledged elephant in the moral salon for centuries. The sheer absurdity of a theology of women's sexuality developed, taught, and enforced exclusively by men has only recently begun to dawn on either the subjects or the objects of this abstract endeavor.[30] Some of the developments discussed in the previous section in relation to women's increasing autonomy in the sphere of sexuality have, without doubt, focused attention on such issues as contraception, abortion, divorce and remarriage, monogamy and marital fidelity, artificial insemination, in vitro fertilization, and others.

Carol Gilligan's groundbreaking book, *In a Different Voice*,[31] questioned the assumption that male moral development and reasoning processes were equivalent to and normative of human functioning in the sphere of morality, which supposedly established scientifically that women's "failure" to think like men was a curious but congenital retardation in their moral development. She investigated empirically how women reason morally and highlighted the ascendancy of concrete relationality over abstract rationality in the process. Although her conclusions have been relativized by subsequent investigation and have needed refinement, Gilligan set in motion a movement within moral theology that met and was reinforced in the Catholic sphere by the move toward personalist rather than physicalist approaches to moral reasoning.[32]

In the sphere of morality, perhaps more pointedly than in any other area, the significance of women's experience surged into prominence. While there is some truth in the claim that Catholic moral theology did not take anyone's experience into account as it reasoned from abstract principles to concrete conclusions undeterred by the psychic and spiritual wreckage it left in its wake, it was male experience that was the unacknowledged substrate of this reasoning process. When moral theologians such as Bernard Häring, Charles Curran, Joseph Fuchs, and Richard McCormick began, in the conciliar era, to focus attention on that unacknowledged substrate, women moral theologians began to point out the fact that women's life experience was not identical to men's, women's approaches to moral reasoning were different in significant respects, and even some of women's moral concerns were quite different. This was true not only in the obvious area of sexuality but in other areas as well.

The significance of this realization goes well beyond the substance of moral theology to reinforce the conclusion coming from other spheres of inquiry that the assimilation of women to men as a subordinate and defective subset of the human norm is a fundamentally mistaken methodological assumption that has skewed all of theology down through the centuries. What is called for is nothing less than a complete revision, in the sense of reexamination, of all of theology, as if the human race had two genders whose experience, though equivalent, is not identical but is equally important. In short, the theological imagination has been shocked into a re-conceiving of the theological enterprise from the ground up.

b. Overall Approach to Theological Scholarship

Several features of the revision of theology that has been underway for at least three decades owe a great deal to the emergence of women in the field, both as practitioners and as sources of relevant data. First, the *category of "the other,"* which was relevant in regard to the poor in Latin American liberation theology, to people of color in Black and Hispanic theology, to Asians in non-Western theology, and to homosexuals within first-world theology was particularly relevant to women because all women are "the other" and many, such as poor women of color, are doubly or triply so because of their membership in more than one oppressed or marginalized group.

The assumption of classical Western philosophy and theology was that humanity was normatively white, Western, male, and Christian. Working out the nature and appropriate relationships of this normative human supplied the basic framework for understanding any and all people who were assumed to be substantially like, even if accidentally different from, this norm. The arrogance and imperialism of this subsuming of everyone else into the white male paradigm and the Western Christian master narrative were invisible to those who thought in these hegemonic categories because, for them, it was not a man-made epistemological paradigm but simply an objective description of reality. Many of the oppressed whose distinctive identity was obliterated by this approach also accepted this hegemony because they lacked the resources to call it into question either theoretically or through political action.

A major difference among women, especially those who had access to education (as was increasingly the case for middle-class white women in the West), and other oppressed groups was that some of the former rapidly acquired the intellectual and academic tools to question the status quo. What European-trained Latin American theologians were able to do with and for the poor, that is, bridge the gap between experience and analysis, educated middle-class women were able to do within the feminist movement, namely, articulate and analyze the experience of oppression and exclusion and thus use the "master's tools," academic and political, to begin dismantling the "master's house," the palace of patriarchy.

Women are quintessentially "the other" to the supposedly normative male. As the popular self-help literature on male-female relationships suggests, they are both fully human and from a different planet.[33] Women are biologically really different from the male, especially because of their awesome capacity to give life. But they are also different, as feminists insist, because of their socialization and experience. A major feature of the feminist movement has been the rejection by large numbers of women of both the attempt to assimilate women to men and the definition of women's differences as inferiority. Women are not defective men; but they are also not simply men in drag. They are "other" and the "difference that difference makes" must begin to be taken into account in everything from the structuring of work schedules and the pattern of career advancement to the way money is allocated for medical research. The category of "the other" is fundamentally changing the overall approach of scholarship to reality. It is moving, with glacial slowness, toward taking into account the fact that reality, especially human reality, is irreducibly plural and not merely hierarchically dualistic.

A second, and related, change in the overall approach to scholarship is the emergence of "*social location*" as a determining condition of all knowing. Again, feminists are not the only scholars who have fostered this development, but they were in the front lines of the battle against Enlightenment "objectivity," the claim of patriarchal scholarship to a universal, unbiased, and politically neutral pursuit of truth and production of knowledge. Feminist scholars have insisted that not only is there no such thing as pre-suppositionless knowledge, but also there is no such thing as nonsituated inquiry. Where one stands determines what one sees. Men do not see reality *tout court;* they see what their male experience allows them to see, even when they are looking at women's life or literature! Furthermore, no inquiry is value-free. Every scholar, whether he or she knows it or not, has an agenda, and all scholarship is, in this sense, interested, that is, political. Someone profits from what is studied, the way knowledge is articulated, how it is made accessible (or restricted), and how it is used in society. This is not a cynical suspicion of jealous academic losers, as many male scholars insisted when feminism first made such claims in the groves of academe. It is a recognition that humans act for a purpose that may be constructive or destructive but is not neutral. By acknowledging and claiming their feminist agenda as the pursuit of a truth that liberates women and other oppressed people, feminists, along with other liberationist scholars, have helped force all scholars out of the closets of pseudo-objectivity and into the political marketplace.

The change in the academy as a result of the recognition of the role of social location has been sometimes subtle but swift and profound. Styles have changed. For example, contemporary academic writers seldom speak in the imperial "we," suggesting disembodied omniscience about their subjects. And they are reticent about using the "divine passive" to suggest that their conclusions are incontrovertible. Rather than "it is clear that..." we read "it seems to me that...." Many authors feel obligated to state explicitly who they are and whence they come and what effect they think that location has had on their work in terms both of access to data and limitation of perspective. Increasingly, publishers insist on the use of inclusive language, which keeps the importance of sexual differentiation on the front burner.

But even more important than changes in style and procedures are such substantive changes as the recognition by scholars, institutions, and fund-granting agencies of the need to include women and people of color on research teams and faculties. A bibliography that takes no account of feminist approaches to a subject marks the writer as out-of-date if not out-of-touch. This increased inclusiveness is no longer seen as a soporific to an angry feminist Cerberus but as an evident necessity for valid research.

A third effect of women's presence in the world of scholarship is the increasingly important role of *interdisciplinarity*. Again, women scholars have not been the initiators or the sole agents of this development. In the postwar decades maverick scientists like Benoit Mandelbrot, trained as a mathematician, who ventured into economics, astronomy, climatology, physics, engineering, and physiology in his groundbreaking explorations of what has come to be called "chaos theory,"[34] pioneered the breakdown of the rigid boundaries that hermetically sealed post-Enlightenment disciplines into their self-contained and self-referential domains. But liberation scholarship in general and feminist scholarship in particular, because it not only studied a particular subject matter such as women's experience but insisted that any and all subject matter, including all the classical areas of theology, could be studied from a feminist perspective, fostered the movement across disciplinary lines. Rosemary Radford Ruether's major work, *Sexism and God-Talk*,[35] was a typical example of a re-visioning of all the branches of theology from the standpoint of feminism.

The feminist critique of society and of scholarship necessitated the mobilization of resources from a plurality of fields. Two methods of doing this emerged. One was to assemble a group of scholars from a variety of fields to work on a single research project, as, for example, Catherine LaCugna did in *Freeing Theology*.[36] The other was for a single researcher or team to draw on material from a variety of fields, as Gilligan did in relation to women's moral development or Belenky and associates did in *Women's Ways of Knowing*,[37] in which psychology, social history, sociology, educational theory, empirical research in actual learning situations, and theoretical construction were brought together to articulate and analyze the cognitive development of women.

Interdisciplinarity, which is certainly the emerging shape of contemporary scholarship, constitutes a kind of reversal of the quintessentially male and patriarchal Enlightenment ideal of scholarship.[38] Analysis for its own sake is giving way to synthesis in the service of social change. The rigid delineation of academic turf, access to which is denied to all but those who have negotiated the appropriate disciplinary rites of passage and whose exclusivity is maintained by jargon unintelligible to the uninitiated, is giving way to a kind of intellectual free migration and an increasing use, even among scholars, of the *lingua franca* of ordinary language.[39] The motivation for research is, increasingly, the desire to respond to real-life questions such as violence or the search for meaning or the possibility of maturity or the conditions of commitment, rather than the construction of esoteric positions on exotic topics that will assure the academic eminence of their inventors. To a large extent these shifts are due to the entrance into the academy of people previously excluded, in many cases women. The marginalized, who did not help to create the Enlightenment academy and who have not profited from its operations, have brought a new agenda into the conversation, which is demanding a whole new approach to knowledge: where it comes from, how it is established, who generates it, and what it is for. Interdisciplinarity responds much better to these concerns than the intellectual inbreeding of the classical academic specializations.

Finally, a development that is closely related to the preceding three and that I will only mention here is the *emergence of spirituality* as a legitimate academic discipline. At first a practical subdivision of pastoral preparation, virtually restricted to Roman Catholic institutions, the study of the experiential interaction between humans and the divine has gradually become a cross-cultural, interreligious (and sometimes nonreligious) research discipline operating under its own name or through a variety of subterfuges in the university setting, both religious and nondenominational. No longer confined to the field of religious development of individuals, spirituality has begun to be invoked as a dimension of the preparation of business executives, doctors and lawyers, educators and scientists.

Again, I would not want to claim that the interest in spirituality, which is one of the preeminent characteristics of contemporary American culture and increasingly in the academy, originated with feminist scholars. But once again, feminism in the academy has played a major role in the development of the interest. From the beginning of feminist scholarship, women have identified the reappropriation of "spirit" as a primary objective of the feminist movement. Spirit, that capacity of the human to transcend nature and create history through the exploits of the intellectual and religious power inherent in humanity, has been assigned to men throughout virtually all of Christian history. Women, by contrast, were thought to be biologically destined to immersion in matter, in bodiliness, in the natural processes of reproduction, food gathering and preparation, providing clothing and shelter against the elements. Their natural sphere was sexuality, children, family, survival, while men's sphere was religious and political leadership, art, research, invention, and world conquest. Feminists realized that accession to full human stature meant accession to spirit. Consequently, feminist spirituality has been integral to feminist thought from the beginning.[40]

Although these four shifts in the approach to scholarship are not the only transformations we are currently seeing in the academy and none of them is due exclusively to the presence or activity of feminist scholars, it seems to me abundantly clear that the influence of feminism has been an imaginative shock of major proportions, precipitating and fostering significant changes in the intellectual life of the first world and its institutional framework. Athletics and scholarship, the arenas of body and spirit, are domains of massive imaginative reorganization, due in large measure to the emergence of real women into these spheres and the development of feminist theory to undergird that practice. As the human enterprise gradually comes to be seen as a two-sex experience, values such as recognition of the other, equality, mutuality, relationality, interdependence, and cooperation are beginning to appear as not only "women's strange ways of being" but as a human way of being that may be preferable to imperialism, domination, rugged individualism, and competition.

CHAPTER TWO
THE EFFECT OF FEMINISM ON THE CHURCH

Having looked at the development of feminism and some of its effects on first-world culture through the change in women's status and the subverting of the patriarchal imagination occasioned by women's entrance into the world of sports and the academy, we are now in a position to inquire into the effects of feminism in the Church. I want to discuss first the influence from without, that is, from cultural feminism, and then examine in some detail a significant influence from within, namely, women's Religious Life and the schools for girls and women founded by women's Religious congregations.

A. THE SECULAR WOMEN'S LIBERATION MOVEMENT AND THE CHURCH

The third wave of the women's movement, the feminism of the second half of the twentieth century, was originally a secular phenomenon. As mentioned above, women involved in the civil rights and the antiwar movements at midcentury began to realize that, despite their total involvement, they were not equal partners in the work, and their protests against their subordinate position were met with indifference or scorn from their male associates who considered the women's concerns trivial in comparison with racial prejudice and militarism. Many men saw no connection between the oppressions they were fighting and the oppression women were experiencing, but women were beginning to see the connection. What linked these causes was patriarchy, the ideology and social structure of domination of the weak by the powerful, whose paradigmatic instance was male control of women. Thus feminist consciousness began to rise among socially active women who had become astute in analysis and practiced in resistance.

The first national leaders in the new wave of women's liberation, women like Gloria Steinem and Betty Friedan, were not religiously motivated, and those like Carol Christ and Christine Downing,[41] who came from within the academy and had a vested interested in spirituality, were very wary of organized religion which was no champion of women's liberation. The first radical Catholic feminists to become public figures were probably Mary Daly, whose *Beyond God the Father*[42] was a trumpet call to Catholic women to wake up to what was happening to them and around them in the Church, and Rosemary Radford Ruether, whose liberationist commitment focused early, although not exclusively, on women in the Church. They pointed to the clear connection between patriarchal theology and sexist oppression and thus began building the bridge between secular feminism and Catholic women who would become committed feminists of the next decades.

1. The Impact of Feminism in Relation to Ministry, Liturgy, and Language

It is always difficult to discern, even in hindsight, the factors that trigger a change of social consciousness. Some possible catalysts for the emergence of feminist consciousness among Catholic women were undoubtedly rooted in the Second Vatican Council itself, which closed in 1965. Women Religious, as a group, especially those in ministerial congregations, were already perhaps the best religiously educated segment among the nonordained, and they were deeply committed to the Church. Eagerly poised to implement the agenda of the Council, they seized upon its profession of the Church's solidarity with contemporary humanity, were deeply moved by its affirmation of the equality of all the baptized in the call to holiness and ministry, and were stimulated by the challenge to reaffirm their own long-suppressed charism as apostolic rather than monastic Religious. Thus women Religious were poised to become a natural conduit of feminist consciousness into the Church.

But almost immediately after the close of the Council, women, especially Religious, began to experience the ambivalence of Church officials in regard to the implementation of conciliar changes, and the contradictions between these ringing affirmations of equality and solidarity and the reality of the patriarchal power structure in the Church. Many women entertained high hopes during and immediately after the Council that the centuries-long exclusion of women from presbyterial ordination would be reexamined and eventually abrogated. Not only was this not to be, but even ordination to the diaconate, despite evidence that women in the early Church had exercised this ministry and the fact that it was now open to married laymen, was declared closed to women. Women were denied equality with laymen in relation to even nonordained ministries. Only years of struggle opened serving at the altar and reading during liturgy to women, and even then only men could be officially installed as acolytes or lectors.

Without doubt, the emergence of the issue of women's ordination and the increasing Vatican resistance to it has done more than anything else to clarify and intensify feminist consciousness among Catholic women. Although some bishops, in the immediate postconciliar years, were open to at least listening to women on the subject, Vatican resistance became more and more entrenched. In 1976, in *Inter Insigniores,* the declaration denying the possibility of the admission of women to orders, it declared the subject closed because, among other reasons, of women's lack of physical resemblance to Jesus as male. This highly offensive and theologically flawed argument not only failed to halt the movement, which by this time had developed its own national organization,[43] but fueled intensive research that exposed the lack of cogency of the arguments. The acceptance of women's ordination among Catholic men as well as women gradually became the majority position within the North American and European Church. The Vatican returned to the subject several times in succeeding years, finally attempting to declare its position infallible and threatening punitive action against anyone who continued to discuss it, much less advocate it.[44] Needless to say, this has in no way lessened the commitment of women's ordination advocates. Rather, it has heightened and intensified feminist consciousness among increasing numbers of women (and men) in the Church, which, reciprocally, has exacerbated Vatican resistance to the entire feminist agenda, which it now clearly sees as the major threat within the Church to patriarchal power.

This escalating and reciprocally reinforced tension between feminist Catholics and the Vatican has become symbolically incarnated in the struggle over inclusive language in official Church discourse. The role of male-generic exclusive language in the marginalization and oppression of women was one of the first realizations of secular feminists,

traception unlawful and sinful.[48] This sounded a warning that the optimism of many Catholics about the Church's engagement with the modern world was perhaps premature if not exaggerated. Although the encyclical was protested by theologians and pastors and was never really "received" by the Catholic faithful,[49] it has remained the official ecclesiastical position, and giving it at least lip service has become a litmus test for episcopal appointment. Statistical data shows that Catholic women practice contraception at about the same rate as non-Catholic women and apparently neither they nor many of their pastors consider this sinful.[50]

In the 1973 U.S. Supreme Court case of *Roe v. Wade*, women obtained the legal right to have an abortion without the consent of their husbands or other male guardians. The Catholic Church has remained adamantly opposed to direct, procured abortion for any reason and has imposed its ultimate sanction of excommunication on anyone who procures or provides an abortion.[51] Although the controversy over this issue rages on in political campaigns, courts, and Congress, it is fairly clear that the majority of Americans, including Catholics, agree that "rape, incest, and threat to the life of the mother" can justify a woman's choice to abort. There is no such consensus around abortion for convenience or as a form of contraception.[52] This consensus and bifurcation in national opinion is quite instructive about the perceived relationship between women's liberation and women's control over their own body-persons as symbolized by their reproductive capacities. There seems to be a growing consensus, even among Catholics who know that their position is not in accord with official Church teaching, that a woman has the right, and even sometimes a duty, to control her participation in the reproductive process insofar as it involves her bodily integrity. This is perceived as a right that is rooted, on the one hand, in the right to self-preservation and, on the other, in immunity from physical violation. A woman, in this view, is free to prevent pregnancy either before voluntary intercourse or immediately after violation by rape. And if she is impregnated against her will, she has the right to refuse to carry such a pregnancy to term. Furthermore, if she must choose between her own life and that of the fetus, even if freely conceived, she may choose self-preservation.[53]

However, many (perhaps even most) who hold this position are much more ambivalent about, or even adamantly opposed to, the use of abortion as a remedy for freely chosen sexual activity, especially promiscuity or sexual irresponsibility. In other words, many people make a real moral distinction between accepting the consequences of the violation of one's person and accepting responsibility for one's freely chosen actions, even if these have unintended and tragic consequences. The latter is an obligation, whereas the former may not be.

The absolute refusal of the official Church to engage the reasoning of the majority of medical or psychological professionals, theologians, married people, and especially women on these questions, despite the Council's affirmation that all the People of God should be involved in the legitimate development of the Church's self-understanding and moral vision and that laity with special expertise or experience (and not only those already in agreement with the official position) should be consulted in the areas of their competence, has hardened the divide between feminist Catholics and the hierarchy. Although some Catholics accept the Church's position on abortion, the resort to punitive power has not convinced anyone who does not accept it of the truth of the official position nor of their own obligation to observe the law or enforce it. It has, unfortunately, exacerbated the awareness of and resistance to the Church's sexual morality in general and seriously weakened the Church's moral leadership in an area that has too few thoughtful and compassionate advocates, namely, the conundrums around life issues that modern technology has generated.

In short, the rise of feminism in secular society has exerted, as it were from the outside, a powerful influence on the institutional Church. Societal issues of equal economic and political opportunity, access to power, social equality, and freedom from heterodetermination, male domination, and sexually based violence have their analogues in the Church in the issues of women's ordination and liturgical participation, inclusive language, and sexual morality, especially as it touches issues of reproduction. But of greater interest for our purposes is the influence of feminism from within the Church.

B. Women's Religious Life as a Resource for the Liberation of Women in the Church

In this section I want to suggest that feminism among Catholic women, although catalyzed by and partially reflective of the secular feminist movement, is actually more indigenous to the Church itself than an import from the surrounding culture. The rising of feminist consciousness and the emergence of feminist activism within the American Church is the eruption of a nonviolent revolution that has been germinating since the eighteenth century and that is deeply rooted in the Gospel and the experience of Catholic women, especially women Religious.

1. The Uniqueness of Roman Catholic Women's Religious Life

Although Catholic Religious Life has analogues in most of the great literate religious traditions of the world and although some of these traditions include women among their devotees, there is really nothing comparable, quantitatively or qualitatively, to women's apostolic Religious Life as it developed in the American Church since the arrival in 1727 of a small group of Ursulines from France in what is now New Orleans.[54] Only quite recently have historians, both ecclesiastical and secular, become interested in unearthing and telling the story of the more than 300,000 women who have lived Religious Life in this country since that first band arrived.[55] That story has been almost entirely submerged in the history of male clerics, who were far fewer in number and whose influence on the faith of the American Church as opposed to its organization, it could be argued, was considerably less deep. The neglect of the history of American women Religious reflects the general defect of modern historiography that feminist historians are trying to redress, namely, that it has tended to equate history with the exploits of those who wield public power, virtually always men, to the neglect of everyone and everything else, especially women.

As the story of women's Religious Life has begun to be told, the uniqueness of the phenomenon is becoming strikingly evident. Religious Life, both male and female, was suppressed at the time of the Protestant Reformation[56] and, with a few notable exceptions, has not yet reemerged in the Protestant communions, although interest among Protestants is increasing and experiments are multiplying. Within Christianity, only Roman Catholicism has nurtured within itself what sociologist Patricia

Wittberg has called a "virtuoso" form of Christian life and commitment for women.[57] Although the notion of religious virtuosity requires considerable nuancing in the context of the equality and universal call to holiness of all the baptized, it is a convenient peg on which to hang the collection of distinctive traits that marks out Religious Life as a specialized (though not superior) Christian lifeform.

Besides its uniqueness in relation to other Christian denominations, women's Religious Life is also distinctive within the Catholic Church in relation to both the laity and the clergy. Historically, that distinction was generally (and unfortunately) perceived in terms of superiority to the laity and assimilation to the clergy. In fact, the distinction is precisely that, in terms of the hierarchical organization of the Church into two classes, ordained and lay, Religious Life is both lay and ministerial. That is, Religious are nonordained (in that sense, lay), and they are actively engaged in the Church's public ministry (though not official representatives of the hierarchy). This paradoxical situation of being not contained within either class of the hierarchical institution places Religious in a potentially prophetic relation to the Church as institution. The prophetic character of the lifeform has sometimes resulted in tension between Religious and the hierarchy, as was the case of the prophets in relation to the kings of Israel and of Jesus in relation to the Jewish hierarchy of his time. Religious are often enough the "loyal opposition" in the Church, calling for fidelity to the Gospel when the political or economic agenda of the institution seems threatened by such fidelity.

This short essay is not the place to develop a full-scale theology of Religious Life as a prophetic phenomenon[58] and I will return to this subject in the final part of this essay. However, it is important at this point to insist that, on the one hand, Religious Life is not a pool of cheap labor for Church institutions. Nor, on the other hand, is the prophet a person with a privileged pipeline to the divine who is privy to God's secrets. The prophet is a person called by God to mediate a three-way interaction among God, culture, and the People of God. The prophet does not have a more direct access to the divine mind, or better knowledge of what we as a Church are called to be and do, but the prophet does have a unique perspective on what is going on.

The prophet's unique perspective arises from a twofold self-situation, on the one hand in relation to God and on the other in relation to society. At the heart of Religious Life is contemplative intimacy with God, who is the exclusive object of affective commitment in the sense that the Religious makes no other primary life commitment, for example, to spouse and family, to profession or career, or to artistic, intellectual, or commercial projects. And by the vows of consecrated celibacy, evangelical poverty, and obedience to God alone, the Religious chooses to remain marginal to the basic dynamics of society in regard to sexuality, wealth, and power. The only question the Religious raises about what is going on in society, whether ecclesial or secular, is about its relationship to the Gospel, to the promotion of the Reign of God. It is not that Religious have the answer to that question, but they help keep the question alive and focused. Often they do so by "living the questions" within their own lives, their experience of persecution by the institutional Church for their solidarity with or ministry to those who have been ecclesiastically marginalized, or their confrontation with civil power over the participation of the poor, issues of life and death in health care and in prisons, war as an instrument of foreign policy, and so on.

Immediacy to God and social marginality constitute a unique "place" from which Religious as individuals and as a lifeform in the Church, raise the question of the Church's fidelity to the Gospel in calling for and helping to build a just society. Like the prophets of the Old Testament in relation to ancient Israel and Jesus in the New Testament in relation to the People of God of his time, Religious, in virtue of public profession, challenge the Church to be what it is called to be, the city seated on a hill, the light to the nations drawing all people to God. This prophetic role is fostered both by the fact that Religious do not make the commitments within and to the secular order that other laity do—the very commitments that are the source of the leverage for change in the secular order which Vatican II recognized as the special contribution of the laity—and by the fact that they are not, like the clergy, official representatives of the hierarchical institution. Often this is misunderstood by both laity and clergy. However, the slowly emerging history of Religious Life in this country as well as the publicity surrounding the ministry of people like Helen Prejean, C.S.J., Theresa Kane, R.S.M., Joan Chittister, O.S.B., and Jeannine Gramick, S.S.N.D., are gradually educating American Catholics and others to the true nature of Religious Life as a prophetic lifeform in the Church. In what follows I will look at three arenas within which this prophetic lifeform has developed resources for the future.

2. Living an Alternative Ecclesiology

No segment of the Catholic population changed more visibly or dramatically in the wake of the Council than women Religious. In one sense, this was due to the fact that this life was encrusted with exotic and esoteric clothes, customs, and practices whose modification or abandonment was publicly visible. Anachronistic habits were replaced with ordinary clothes, cloistered convents were opened or replaced by ordinary dwellings, and an agrarian horarium was brought into relation with the modern timetable of ordinary adults. But at a much deeper and more substantive level, the visible changes in

Religious Life were reflected by the surfacing of an ecclesiology that was both more in tune with the ideal the Council articulated and strikingly different from that which the institutional Church had, at least since the Reformation, embodied.

Women's Religious Life, partly because no members, being women, held ecclesiastical office and thus enjoyed "ontological" superiority to others in the community, was always in principle egalitarian.[59] Even superiors had transitory authority delegated to them by ecclesiastical officials who retained the right to withdraw it. This did not prevent authoritarianism and abuse of power in women's Religious orders, but it did preserve, deep in the structure of the life itself, the vision of the Gospel community as a discipleship of equals in which there were to be no fathers or masters lording it over the others but only sisters and brothers of Jesus, children of one God (cf. Mt 23:6–11).

Freed of centuries of quasi-clerical encrustation women's Religious Life rapidly reformed itself in the direction of egalitarian discipleship. The class structure of choir and lay sisters was abolished. Leadership was reinterpreted as a shared charism involving all members in the direction of the community's life and mission. Officeholders ceased to exercise unaccountable power, and mutual discernment regarding ministries, living situations, and most other aspects of life replaced unilateral, top-down decision making. In short, collegiality, subsidiarity, dialogue, and co-responsibility became the principles of community life. The rapid transformation of Religious congregations from hierarchical power structures in the image of the centralized ecclesiastical institution into communities of equals more resonant of the ideal expressed in Acts 4:32-35 met considerable opposition from the Vatican as it received for approval the revised constitutions of various orders. But women Religious have persevered in their agenda of evangelical self-transformation.

The reformation of structures has allowed certain aspects of Religious community that were obscured in preconciliar times to reappear. In particular, the nature of Religious Life as a voluntary community based on the principle of "from each according to her ability and to each according to her need" was reaffirmed. Equality among members was seen less as absolute uniformity in lifestyle and possessions as well as in ministry and relationships and more as an individualized participation in a common life and project. Community life came to be seen as fully compatible with diversity of ministries, living situations, and even lifestyles. Individuality and community, now distinguished from individualism and collectivism, are increasingly seen as mutually reinforcing rather than competitive.

The increased interaction among members within Religious congregations led rapidly to broadened relationships with people outside their communities. Religious began to network with members of other congregations, with like-minded and committed laity, and with people of other faiths, especially in the work of justice and peace. This has encouraged a re-evaluation of personal friendships that are no longer seen as a threat to community but as an enhancement of the person and an enrichment of the group. And this has fostered, on the one hand, a virtual explosion of different forms of relationship of laity with Religious congregations as associates, oblates, or volunteers in ministry and, on the other hand, ongoing relationships with non-Catholic Christians and people of other religions or no religion. The Council's challenge to break down the barriers between Catholics and the rest of the world moved much more rapidly among Religious than it did in the official ecumenical and interreligious dialogues established by the hierarchy.

The nonclerical nature of Religious ministry, once the virtual equation of Religious ministry with the running of ecclesiastical institutions was broken, led inevitably to Religious reassuming their pioneer function in the Church.[60] Women Religious began to serve not only in parishes but as chaplains in prisons and hospitals, as NGO representatives at the United Nations, in ministry to the homosexual community, to the victims of AIDS, to women who have had abortions or been victims of rape or domestic abuse, or wherever societal or ecclesiastical dynamics marginalize or victimize people. Again, this development among women Religious has, often enough, been viewed with suspicion by the very Church officials who participated in Vatican II and formulated the challenge to be in these very places and do these very tasks.

In short, the Council allowed Religious Life to reemerge as a particular way of being Church that is egalitarian, nonhierarchical, and interactive across boundaries of denominations, states of life, and religions or cultures. It has rediscovered its call to be nurturing of individuals in community, totally but diversely ministerial, pioneering, and prophetic. Especially since the Council, Religious have been living an ecclesiology that many people see as the ideal proposed by the Gospel. Because it is sometimes in stark contrast to the highly centralized and often morally condemnatory ethos of the institutional Church, there is a frequently erupting tension between women Religious and the Vatican, which has occasionally developed into actual conflict and confrontation, yet this has also created a place and space where many people alienated from other institutional expressions of Church have been able to find acceptance and refuge.

3. Developing a Corps of Professional Women in the Church

The emerging history of Religious congregations in this country bears witness to the extraordinary initiative, resourcefulness, and leadership of women Religious, especially in the century and a half preceding Vatican II, in the founding, administering, and staffing of institutions to serve, at first, the poor immigrant Catholic population and, later, culturally assimilated middle-class Catholics and their non-Catholic contemporaries. Between 1829 and 1990, for example, women Religious founded approximately 845 hospitals and, up to the present, over 300 colleges. An enormous number of grammar and high schools in virtually every diocese in the country was staffed by Sisters who educated millions of American children.[61] At the same time that this prodigious work was taking place in the United States, Religious congregations were sending thousands of Sisters to over fifty different mission countries, where they established, administered, and staffed schools, dispensaries, hospitals, and agencies of social service.

A major difference between the apostolic works undertaken by women Religious and those initiated by male Church personnel was the tenuousness of the material support available to the women. Only in the last decade has the institutional Church in this country recognized the extent of the financial exploitation, unintentional no doubt but very real, of women Religious who worked oppressively long days and often nights without vacations or even weekends of respite for very little financial recompense and with no provision for health insurance or retirement benefits. Schools ran on bake sales and raffles, in-kind contributions from parents and parishioners, and the willingness of the Sisters to serve not only as teachers and administrators of their institutions but also as child-care providers, cooks, and janitors.

While the largely unrequited use of women Religious is not a credit to the American hierarchy, it nevertheless necessitated the self-development of Religious in this country into the best-trained and educated group of Catholic women anywhere in the Church. The institutions women Religious founded needed educated and, eventually, professionally credentialed personnel. For decades Sisters were routinely sent into classrooms and even operating rooms with abysmally inadequate training, and the process for educating Sisters was often haphazard and even chaotic. Religious were, on the one hand, the victims of their own success, because bishops and pastors would not recognize the need for education of the Sisters who were obviously doing an outstanding job without it. On the other hand, pastors with hundreds of children in their parish schools were adamantly opposed to being deprived of "their" Sisters long enough for them to be adequately educated. Furthermore, Religious superiors themselves, no matter how committed to the education of their members (and not all were) perpetually found themselves hard-pressed to secure the necessary funds for higher education of their members, especially as this very education removed a significant group of earners from the classroom and stretched the remaining personnel ever more thinly.

Nevertheless, there was a growing realization that if Religious were to maintain their institutions in an increasingly competitive market, their personnel had to be as well prepared as their lay counterparts.[62] Increasingly, even before the launching of the Sister Formation Movement, whose *magna carta* was formulated by Sister Madeleva Wolff in 1949, Sisters were being sent to college, to nursing school and normal school, and on for graduate degrees. The Sister Formation Movement stressed not only the professional preparation of Religious but the integration of their intellectual, psychological, social, and spiritual growth as persons. Although most Religious were being educated to teach in the secular sciences and humanities, they were also beginning to study college-level theology. They were being taught not only by priests brought in for this purpose, but also by the first women to undertake graduate theological study, beginning in this country at Saint Mary's College, Notre Dame, Indiana, in 1943 with the establishment of the graduate School of Sacred Theology, and at the Regina Mundi Institute, established in Rome in 1954. It is highly significant that women Religious, unlike their diocesan clerical counterparts, were being educated not only in the undergraduate liberal arts, philosophy, and theology, but in the humanities, the social and personality sciences, the physical sciences, and the professions. The greater intellectual and spiritual readiness of women Religious to undertake the implementation of Vatican II was due in large measure to this population's extensive preparation in both human and sacred studies coupled with intensive personal and spiritual formation.

Aside from their formal formation, intellectual and spiritual, women Religious were also the beneficiaries of a remarkable mentorship system within their own orders. Through daily life in the convent, they learned from older Sisters (and often overly demanding superiors) the importance of hard work and efficiency, of self-discipline and the ability to delay gratification, of responsibility and generosity, of being accountable and expecting accountability of one another, of cooperation and collaboration, and of the crucial role spiritual motivation played in such a rigorous lifestyle. In their institutions they were initiated by more experienced Religious into their professional duties, encouraged to competence and even excellence, not for self-aggrandizement but for the sake of the Reign of God. They learned to lead as well as follow. And as soon as they were ready, many were placed, even at relatively young ages, into positions of responsibility that the vast majority of women would never have the opportunity to fill. They were hospital and nursing school administrators, school principals and college presidents, as well as primary school experts, professors, health care and social workers.

Increasingly, as Sisters filled important professional roles, they began to participate in and even lead professional organizations, which resulted in a vast networking not only with other Religious but also with lay colleagues, both Catholic and non-Catholic. These connections would be increasingly important in the aftermath of the Council, when the numbers of Religious declined steeply and the institutional culture of preconciliar convent life was dismantled. One of the most important instruments of networking among Religious themselves is the Leadership Council of Women Religious, formally inaugurated in 1956,[63] which brings together the leaders of about 95 percent of American women Religious (approximately 79,000). The LCWR has given congregational leaders not only the forum for mutual encouragement, sharing of resources, and development of corporate ministerial initiatives, especially in the area of justice, but also has provided a certain amount of leverage with ecclesiastical authorities that none of them could exercise individually.

In short, women's Religious life in the American Church has been a remarkable "women's movement" born not of a sense of disempowerment or oppression but of call and power to meet the exigencies of their time, to incarnate their love of God in service of the neighbor. When that movement was infused with the rising consciousness emerging from the secular women's movement, it expanded and deepened but has not lost its distinctive character of commitment, not only to the building of a better world in which women are equal participants, but also to fostering the Reign of God in which all creatures will experience the *shalom* of God.

4. The Education of Women

One of the earliest and most enduring ministries undertaken by women Religious was the education of girls and women. Besides the parochial schools, in which girls and boys were educated together, Religious founded numerous academies and high schools for girls. Some of these gave rise to Catholic women's colleges, while other colleges were founded independently. In a forthcoming volume to be entitled *Beyond the Seven Sisters: Historical Perspectives on Colleges Founded by Women Religious,* the editors note that over three hundred colleges, that is, slightly more than half the women's colleges in the United States, were founded by women's Religious congregations and that they have educated millions of students.[64] Since the turbulence in society and Church of the 1960s, some of these colleges have closed; some have become coeducational; some have partnered with men's institutions; some have evolved into universities; and some have continued as exclusively women's undergraduate institutions. It is well beyond the scope of this essay, and my competence, to supply even a summary history of these secondary schools and colleges, but I want to make one point pertinent to the present argument: women Religious, through these institutions, passed their own vision of women, Church, society, and life in Christ on to successive generations of Catholic women, creating a cadre of well-prepared women who are having and will continue to have a major impact on both the Church and society.

As the editors of *Beyond the Seven Sisters* note, women's colleges were founded by Religious communities for two different purposes. Many were founded for the daughters of lower- and middle-class families that had never included a college graduate. These institutions often emphasized religious formation, business education, teaching, and nursing to prepare their graduates for their roles in the family as wives and mothers, equip those who had to work to earn their livelihood in traditional feminine occupations, and train some to contribute to the traditionally feminine professions. Others, like Saint Mary's in South Bend and Saint Mary-of-the-Woods in Terre Haute, Indiana, Manhattanville and College of New Rochelle in New York, Saint Catherine in Minnesota, Trinity in Washington, D.C., and Marygrove in Michigan, had the same agenda as their more prestigious secular analogues in the Northeast, which were founded to afford women the same high-level education that was available to men at such universities as Georgetown, Notre Dame, or Harvard. Such colleges offered full programs in the liberal arts, and many of their graduates went on to earn higher degrees and become part of the first generation of women in higher education and the professions. But both kinds of Catholic colleges for women lacked the financial resources of the better endowed secular institutions, or even Catholic institutions for men, and this partly explains the fact that they have, until very recently, been virtually ignored in historical studies of higher education in this country and even of higher education for women.

The founding of colleges for women was not generally supported by the Catholic hierarchy, which regarded women as destined for homemaking and family life, for which postsecondary education, presumably, was not needed. And such education was likely to subvert the traditional position that a Catholic wife was to be subject to her husband and devote herself to self-sacrificing service of him and their children. In this, Catholic leadership shared the opinion—widespread in turn-of-the-century America—about the nature, place, and role of women in society. Consequently, the decision of women Religious to forge ahead in this venture was, as in so many other areas, a pioneering venture into uncharted territory.

The history of this venture is paradoxical and fascinating. Women Religious did not see themselves as rebels challenging a restrictive Church structure. If anything, they saw themselves as favored and devoted daughters of the Church, imbued with its values and fully committed to its agenda. As Barbara Johns, I.H.M., of Marygrove College points out in her analysis of the education of young women at Immaculata High School in Detroit, her order's flagship secondary institution for girls from the 1940s to the 1980s, the consciously formulated purpose of the institution, which was typical of such high schools and colleges, was to form Catholic girls in the image of Mary Immaculate.[65]

The Sisters shared the Church's and society's assumption that the proper sphere for a woman was home and family, for which students could prepare by courses in religion and home economics. But they also offered a well-developed college preparatory curriculum, music and art, physical education, and commercial subjects. In other words, as Johns says, "The women's education offered at Immaculata... was, in many ways, a picture of ambivalence."[66] The protofeminist subtext under the sincere espousal of traditional Catholic pieties about the nature and role of women was supplied by the lives and accomplishments of the highly motivated, talented, well-educated, non-married Religious women who staffed the school. While articulating the standard expectations for Catholic women, the Religious were modeling something quite different.

A number of their students entered the congregation upon graduation to take up the life and join in the mission they had come to admire in their teachers. The majority of the others went on to higher education, very often in Catholic women's colleges, and many became civic and educational leaders in the city of Detroit and beyond. They not only had learned the traditional virtues of women but also had imbibed a concern for justice and a commitment to service beyond the sphere of family. They had heard the official message that men, not women, were called to leadership but, in fact, they had become leaders in a school that had no male students to whom to defer. They studied traditional female subjects, but they were also introduced to the classics, the sciences and arts, and to the social encyclicals of the Church. Not only were they not pressured to underachieve in deference to male egos, they were encouraged to excel and were held to high standards of both academic achievement and personal integrity.

This story of ambivalence, of a surface text of feminine inferiority and a subtext of female excellence, was replicated all over the country in women's high schools and colleges. I would hazard the guess that when the story of women's education in Catholic institutions founded by women Religious is finally told, it will be clear that the enthusiastic embrace of the feminist agenda by twentieth-century Catholic women, especially women Religious and their former students, is rooted more deeply in the culture of Religious congregations and the schools for women they founded than in the liberal agenda of the secular women's movement. From the latter these women took the tools of analysis and the strategies for action, but the basic commitment to full person-hood in the image of Jesus Christ for themselves and all creatures emerged from their particular lived experience of the Gospel in the company of women.

CHAPTER THREE
LOOKING TO THE FUTURE

Despite the seduction to prognostication that the turn of the century and the millennium exerts, the rapidity and chaotic character of change in American culture should convince us that we cannot predict the future; we can only create it. Using the resources discovered or developed over the past two centuries and especially since the cultural emergence of the third wave of feminism and the ecclesial cataclysm of the Second Vatican Council, what can we hope to create in this new century? Specifically, can feminism in general and the religiously committed feminism of Christian women and their partners in particular make a positive contribution to the future of the human family and our universe, or is it destined to be suppressed or to fade away, leaving the world still structured by patriarchy, torn by violence, divided between the haves and the have nots, and driven by individualism, greed, and hedonism? Obviously, I think there is hope or I would not be writing this essay. But I do not confuse Christian hope with easy optimism. There is nothing inevitable or predetermined about the emergence of the Reign of God in our midst. We must analyze in depth the challenge we face and marshal the resources at our command if we are to make progress toward a preferred future.

A. ANALYZING THE CHALLENGE OF FEMINIST RECONSTRUCTION OF SOCIETY AND CHURCH

Although there are many aspects and levels to the problem of societal and ecclesial transformation according to the feminist ideal, whether secular or religious, it might be that the most intractable is that of defining the goal itself. In the abstract, the goal is the full personhood of each human being in the service of right relations among all creatures. But what do we mean by full personhood? More specifically, what do we mean by full personhood for women? And what do we mean by right relations?

1. The Conundrum of the Feminist Agenda: Liberation as Equality

Two aspects of the feminist ideal present us with a conundrum. The first has to do with the very notion of equality; the second with the definition of feminism itself. Feminism, in both the societal and the ecclesial spheres, is firmly committed to the equality of persons, and especially equality between women and men. No feminist doubts that the superiority, normativity, dominative power, and privilege of men in relation to women must be definitively terminated. But what would genuine equality between the sexes look like?

In North America the tendency is to conceive equality in terms of individual subjectivity. The rights and duties of the person, based on her or his dignity as an individual human being, are considered in abstraction from the relationships in which she or he is involved. Women should enjoy all the freedoms, rights, protections, opportunities accorded to individual persons in this society but hitherto accorded only to men, who, in fact, were the only ones who *could* abstract from their relationships. In most other societies, including some in first-world Europe, the tendency has been to define equality more in terms of equity, taking into account the "difference that difference makes," and especially the differences that arise from relationships. Women and men, in this view, are equivalent but not identical. Men, for instance, do not give birth, and this is a monumental difference between the sexes. Should the structure of employment, for example, including promotion and pay, which has hitherto never had to take into account pregnancy, childbirth, and care of small children because the employees were all men, be simply applied to women? Or should it be adjusted, in the name of real equality, to the different but equal situations of women and men? In other words, is there a

way to understand gender difference and consequently to structure the world of work, not as if
women's reality were a deviation from the male
norm and that taking account of women's reality
were a condescension to her inferiority, but as if
humanity were normatively twofold, male and
female, and all human structures needed to reflect
and accommodate both equally?

This issue of whether to incorporate difference
into the ideal of equality is a conundrum in a culture that has heavily weighted the age-old tension
between person and community toward the pole of
individuality. Indeed, individualism, the ideological
corruption of respect for individuality, is a besetting
problem of our society. It resounds in our struggles
over abortion, euthanasia, capital punishment,
genetic testing, mandatory military service, the
educational mainstreaming of handicapped children, immigration, taxation, and dozens of other
societal problems and is exacerbated when the tension resonates in the sphere of sexual diversity. It is
difficult to see how undistorted communication,
much less actual structural change, in relation to
this issue can take place unless we can develop a
way of imagining difference that is nondualistic
and nonhierarchical. Much in our cultural and
educational tradition, to say nothing of our religious
tradition, militates against such imaginative revision.
But it is probably safe to say that such revision will not
be initiated by the historical victors. It will begin,

if it does, with the marginalized and the oppressed, and this suggests that women must play a major role in the project.

The second aspect of the conundrum of equality is the struggle over the definition and therefore the goal of feminism. How feminism is understood significantly shapes the agenda for transformation. The spectrum of definitions is wide, but I will mention only a few by way of example. Contemporary feminism will always be in debt to Mary Daly for her thorough analysis of patriarchy within the Church and the academy. But not everyone agrees with her *separatist* strategy for overcoming it. Should women retreat or, more exactly, advance in exodus, even temporarily, out of patriarchy into an all-female world? Enticing as this can seem when patriarchy is especially oppressive, many women see it as a kind of mirror image of the male model. Aside from its biological and social impracticality, it seems, even in principle, to be more useful as a *Herland* utopian myth to nourish the imagination than as an effective strategy for transformation.[67]

At the other end of the spectrum, Pope John Paul II sincerely believes that he is the true champion of women's liberation, understanding much better than women do what it means to be a real woman and called by his office to explain the ideal. His espousal of the archetype of the eternal feminine and the resulting dual anthropology, which defines woman generically in terms of her vocation to motherhood, grounds an irreducible and unequal "complementarity" between male and female. It exalts the ideal of woman at the expense of real women. Many of those real women, even as they recognize the sincerity of the Pope's desire to promote the dignity of women, know that as long as men define "woman's nature," delineate her appropriate spheres of action, and transmute her destiny as a human being into a biologically sealed feminine fate, women will never be truly equal participants in the human project. The Pope's *romantic feminism* sentences women to perpetual social and religious inferiority and dependence on, if not domination by, men through the lofty rhetoric of spiritual superiority, which projects onto women disproportionate responsibility for human morality while assigning to men the only real agency in the public sphere. Few feminists, Catholic or otherwise, can or will accept this vision of a transformed social order because, in fact, it supports the patriarchal agenda by encouraging women to interiorize and sacralize their inferiority and disempowerment as God's will for their sex.

Somewhere between separatism and romanticism lies *liberal feminism*, which is committed to full equality of women with men in every aspect of life in family, society, and Church. So far, this version of feminism has claimed the allegiance of most women whose consciousness has been raised. The right to vote, access to public office, equal pay for equal work, equal opportunity in the workplace and in the classroom, equality on the playing field and in the locker room, control of their own sexuality and reproductive capacity, equal access to and terms in both marriage and divorce, equality in child rearing responsibilities, equal access to theological education and ordination, freedom from rape and domestic abuse, equality before the law, equal attention to women's health in both research and care are among the issues that claim most of the energy of liberal feminists in our society. However, a variety of signs of the times are calling even this apparently self-evident understanding of feminism into question.

Within the Church, the struggle between the Women's Ordination Conference and Women-Church Convergence over the issue of ordination is emblematic. The once obvious goal of equal access for women to presbyterial ministry has been problematized by a deeper analysis of the clerical system as primarily a sexual power structure, which some feminists believe cannot be reformed but only dismantled. Some women do indeed want to be ordained in the hope that they will be able to reform the hierarchical structure of the Church from within the system. An increasing number of women, however, wonder if this is not equivalent to marrying an alcoholic in order to reform him from within the relationship or, even worse, a case of reinforcing a dysfunctional system by masking problems that will only become evident if new candidates cannot be attracted to it.[68]

The same types of dilemmas are becoming evident in the secular sphere. Is it really a cause for rejoicing that women have been incorporated into military academies where they can now engage in the same degrading brutality toward underclassmen that men have traditionally inflicted on women? Is going into combat to obliterate one's fellow human beings a valid goal for women? Should women have felt some pride when Mohammed Ali's daughter, Leila, on the eve of her first boxing match, declared that her goal was not just to win the contest but to batter her opponent into unconsciousness? Is the increasing number of women incarcerated for violent crimes a sign of increasing social equality? Will we have arrived when women are as emotionally capable of abandoning their children or beating them to death as men have been? In short, it is not at all clear that feminism defined as identification with or imitation of the oppressor is a truly liberating or transforming ideal.

Both aspects of the conundrum, defining equality and defining feminism's goals, suggest that this first phase of the feminist contribution to a transformed Church and world may be coming to a close. What seemed self-evident, in regard to both the ends and the means, is no longer so clear. We are being challenged to deepen our analysis, to refocus our agenda, and to refine our strategies.

2. The Heart of the Problem: Moving beyond the Dualisms

It seems to me that one of the major outcomes of our struggles over gender in the twentieth century, especially in the first world, has been a deepening of the gender relationship question itself. We may have exhausted the transformative potential of the discussion carried on in terms of equality (even though that valid agenda has not yet been achieved and the work must continue) and are being invited to plunge deeper into the issue. As in other areas of thought and action, including theology, the dualistic categories that defined problems and staked out the terrain of potential answers in the modern framework are breaking down. The clear-cut distinctions between transcendence and immanence, body and psyche, nature and history, matter and spirit, absolute and relative are increasingly difficult to maintain and progressively less clarifying, even if or when someone finds a nuanced way to keep them functioning in a discussion. The same thing seems to be happening in relation to fundamental dualities which structure the social-sexual paradigm within which we try to understand ourselves as gendered beings and society and Church as the forums for relationships among such beings.

Feminists have long since repudiated the stereotyping dualities that, on the level of individual psychology, assigned intelligence, initiative, leadership, creativity, and most other qualities associated with history and spirit to men and intuition, dependence, emotion, immersion in the body, and most qualities associated with nature and matter to women. Even gender scales, which recognized that some men and some women exhibit traits more characteristic of the other sex, have been exposed as androcentric constructions often functioning as tools of patriarchy.[69]

However, we continue to struggle over the polarity between self-assertion and self-negation and their respective functions in society. Traditionally, women have been expected to carry the dependent/unifying function in society and men the independent/creative function. Without the first, the family and larger society would disintegrate. Without the second, it would stagnate. So women must keep the hearth fires burning to nurture and comfort the men who tame the wilderness and invent the future, and between them they build and maintain an orderly world at both the microcosmic and macroscosmic levels.

Feminists, especially those involved in the personality and social sciences, have exposed this dualistic paradigm, whether individually or socially applied, as dysfunctional, not only for women but for men. The personal merging, submersion of aspirations, self-diffusion, and self-negation assigned to women is clearly a male creation of a support system for themselves and does not express the nature or serve the interests of women.[70] It is infantilizing at best and obliterating at worst. But the compulsive separation and hermetically sealed independence assigned to men is equally dehumanizing. It canonizes a fixation in selfishness, which arrests development in men and which women are no longer willing to tolerate as "just the way men are."

The question, it seems, is what can mediate the tension between self-sacrifice for the good of others and of the whole on the one hand and self-assertion for the good of the self and of society on the other. How can all of us, women and men, individually and collectively, balance care of self and care for others? When should my desires and ambitions, even my real needs, be sacrificed for those of another, and when is such sacrifice an unhealthy exercise in masochism? How do appropriate dependence and healthy independence come together in the interdependence that both knits the human family together and provides the springboard for personal and social development? These tensions exist not only in the family, where spouses must negotiate their relationship with each other, with their children, and increasingly with their aging parents, but also in society, where the issue of taxation is fraught with the dynamics of personal greed versus societal need and immigration policy is caught between nationalist protectionism and compassion, or at the international level, where multinational expansionism is causing desperate poverty and incessant warfare for native populations. I think that the tension between care for the self and service of others is the right question, but I am not at all sure that psychological theories or even social or political ones can supply sufficient resources to address it. The response, which is not simply a reply but a vast challenge, is the establishment of justice in the biblical sense of universal right relationships founded in shared creaturehood and, for Christians, participation in the salvation offered in Jesus to all people.

3. The Gospel as Primary Resource for Christian Prophetic Leadership

Justice in the biblical sense is not a system of retaliation that rebalances a fragile social structure by compensating wrongs in kind, nor merely a quest for quantitative or even qualitative equality. Over the long history of Israel's struggle with God and through the experience of Jesus, to which the New Testament witnesses, the People of God have been slowly initiated into the divine conception of justice. Justice means universal right relationship. But it has taken the new science of the late twentieth century to give us a real insight into the scope and depth of this conception. Quantum physics has shown those who are willing to deal with the evidence that there is no absolute, free-standing reality. The flutter of a butterfly's wing in the heart of Africa actually affects the weather in North

America.[71] Everything is related to everything in a vast network of interdependence. This radically changes the liberal understanding of "enlightened self-interest," according to which, if each takes care of her- or himself, everyone eventually profits. Everything in the cosmos is of concern to me, and I am of concern to everything else. Creation is such that it cannot attain its God-given finality piece-meal. Either we all get to the Promised Land together as a people, or none of us does. Purely private good is an obsolete category.

a. Christianity's Prophetic Vocation

Christianity, like its founding figure Jesus, is an essentially prophetic religion. Both contemporary biblical spirituality and theologically informed studies of culture concur in reappropriating the Old Testament category of prophecy to talk about what Christianity is called to be and to do in the third millennium. Christendom is long dead. And the Church as lifestyle enclave is no longer necessary or compelling.[72] Unless Christianity can make a substantive contribution to the project of universal justice, the tradition has outlived its usefulness. I want to suggest that such a contribution is possible if the example and power of Jesus are incarnated in the prophetic life and mission of Christians in our time.

The prophet, as already mentioned, is neither a fortune-teller nor a divine emissary ranting against the evils of individuals and society. The prophet is a mediator of the ongoing three-way interaction among God, people, and culture.[73] Because culture is continually developing, the prophetic task will never be completed. It is the perpetual challenge of the Church. When Vatican II recognized that the Church is not a hermetically sealed perfect society providing refuge for the saved, within but ideally untouched by "this world," but rather an intimate participant in history through its members who are simultaneously citizens of both Church and world, it actually defined the Church as prophetic. Christians are, or should be, a locus of the encounter between God and the world, as was Jesus, and they are to be neither totally passive nor unilaterally active in this process.

Christians have always had a difficult time imagining this prophetic task. In its first centuries the Church was either a small, persecuted minority trying to survive on the fringe of the Empire by steadfast refusal to participate, or an over-accommodated official organ of the Empire largely submerged in a basically pagan culture. In the Middle Ages culture and Church coincided in the phenomenon of Christendom, which not only ran Europe but felt called to conquer for the faith every new territory discovered. In the modern period the Church ghettoized itself once again, not because it was a persecuted minority, but because it judged the world of modern science and progress godless and perhaps even irredeemable. In hindsight none of these self-situations of the Church in relation to culture, with the possible exception of the medieval, has proven very successful. The Church still oscillates between apologizing for the mistakes and violence of the past and making new and equally violent mistakes in the present.

The problem has been a corporate version of the self-negation versus self-assertion dialectic. The Church has most often either removed itself from culture, been assimilated to culture, or subsumed culture into itself. The tensive prophetic relationship, that is, genuine, ambiguity-ridden, two-way, Gospel-infused cultural participation, is something we as a Church community have not yet managed to imagine into existence. And when some person or some local community does manage it, the result is often enough martyrdom or suppression. The Church can deal with Mother Teresa but not with Jeannine Gramick; it can embrace Opus Dei but struggles with liberation theology. One might say that the Church is either stereotypically male, fiercely independent and even condemnatory of culture, refusing any entangling commitments to it, or stereotypically female, merged to the point of innocuous invisibility into its cultural surroundings. Critical participation, that is, a genuinely prophetic presence, is difficult to sustain.

b. Jesus as Prophetic Model

Although it is well beyond the scope of this essay to explore the Gospel as a whole, I would like to suggest that certain features of its presentation of Jesus are directly relevant to this seemingly insoluble problem of how to imagine the kind of justice for which a new century calls if we are to get beyond the dualistic categories of patriarchy and the conundrums of equality understood in terms of liberal self-interest. Jesus, as the Gospels present him, was a prophet, that is, a mystic rooted in a profound and immediate experience of God, which energized his active commitment to the integral salvation of his contemporaries.[74] He was a true self, an embodiment of personhood incarnated in right relationships. I think it is not insignificant that Jesus is presented in the Gospels as a celibate and a layman, that is, as a man who was not assimilated into the patriarchal gender arrangements that controlled both the social structure and the ecclesial community of his time. He thus remained free to deal with both men and women as his equals. The patriarchalization of the Jesus tradition that began almost immediately after his death cannot point to the Gospel for validation.

Four global features that characterize Jesus' critical participation in his culture might give us some indication of what a truly prophetic stance might look like. To start at the end, Jesus, in the ultimate act of self-abnegation, *gave his life for his fellow human beings but without losing himself.* This was not a challenge he faced for the first time on the cross. Throughout his public life Jesus experienced, suffered from, and negotiated again and again the tension between his own rights and legitimate needs and the insistent demands of others. Repeatedly, the Gospels tell us that Jesus was pursued by the crowds even after he had spent days meeting their physical and spiritual needs (cf. Mk 6:54-56; Jn 6:22 ff.); that even his solitary prayer was interrupted by the needs of his followers and disciples (cf. Mt 14:13-14, 23-25); that he sometimes did not even have time to eat, so insistent were the demands made upon him (cf. Mk 3:20). The crowds pressed him so closely that he could not even identify the recipient of power he felt go out from him (cf. Mk 5:25-34); he sometimes even had to put out from the shore in a boat in order to preach without being crushed (cf. Mt 13:2). And Jesus not only gave to others; he received from them, which is often even more challenging for the rugged individual. He broadened his religious and social categories and even his sense of mission when he met indisputable faith in gentiles (cf. Mk 7:24-30; Mt 8:10). He reached out to his arch-enemies by accepting even their qualified and self-serving hospitality (cf. Lk 7:36-50). He cast his lot with the religiously and socially marginalized (e.g., Jn 7:53–8:11; Mt 9:10-14). And yet, it is clear that Jesus never lost his personal power, the rootedness in God that drew people to him and fascinated even his enemies. Jesus was, apparently, a remarkably centered individual, but his center was God, not his own ego. Jesus gave himself totally, even unto death; but he did not lose himself.

Second, Jesus negotiated the tension between his ancestral faith, that is, his religious tradition, on the one hand, and his mystically rooted prophetic spirituality on the other. *He both belonged to and transcended his tra-dition.* Nowhere in the Gospels do we find Jesus repu-diating his Jewish tradition. He was circumcised into the covenant people and taken up to Jerusalem when he reached the age of responsibility to the Law (cf. Lk 2:21 and 41-42). In his inaugural prophetic trial he replied to the devil's temptations by quoting Deuteronomy, that biblical meditation on the Law of Israel (cf. Lk 4:1-12). He went regularly to syna-gogue, read and preached on the scriptures (cf. Lk 4:19-21). He kept Passover and went up to Jerusalem for the great feasts (see, e.g., Jn 2:13; 5:1; 7:2-10; 10:22-23; 12:1). When asked what salvation required, he responded by citing the command-ments (cf. Mt 19:16-19) and taught that the whole Law and the prophets depended upon the two great commandments of love of God and neighbor (cf. Mt 22:36-40). He respected the Law and its officials (cf. Mt 8:4) and insisted that his disciples do the same, even when those officials were unworthy of their office (cf. Mt 23:2-3). At his transfiguration he appeared between Moses and Elijah, symbols of the Law and the Prophets (Mt 17:3-4). His dying words are quotations from the Psalms (Mt 27:46 and Mk 15:34 citing Ps 22:2 in Hebrew and Aramaic).

Nevertheless Jesus was executed by the Romans on charges brought against him by the officials of Judaism. Jesus broke the law of the Sabbath when his prophetic consciousness called him to do good and to save life (see, e.g., Lk 13:1-17). He cleansed the

Temple when its guardians made it a den of commerce (Jn 2:13-17). He threatened the Temple when it was invoked as a shield for infidelity to God (cf. Mt 23:37-24:2). He excoriated the religious officials who connived with the wealthy and condemned the poor (Mk 12:40-44), who imposed unbearable religious burdens upon the already oppressed (Mt 23:4), who condemned those they considered "sinners" and exalted their own virtue (Lk 18:9-14), who gave themselves religious titles and claimed seats of honor in the religious assembly (cf. Mt 23:5-7), who arrogated to themselves the administration of God's justice (e.g., Jn 7:53—8:11). Jesus did not oppose his personal spirituality to his religious tradition but expressed his spirituality through his religious practice, even as he freely criticized the religious institution out of his own experience of union with God. No one controlled Jesus' access to and relationship with God, but he was able to make his spirituality a resource for the reform of his tradition rather than an alternative to it. Jesus, in other words, belonged truly and deeply to his religious tradition but was neither merged with it nor imprisoned by it.

Third, Jesus mediated the tension between *the particularity of his life and situation and the universality of his concern* through the category of the Reign of God. One of the abiding scandals of Christianity has been the human particularity of Jesus, the Son of God. Jesus was totally situated, as are all healthy human beings who do not attempt escape into nonaffiliation.

He was one person with a particular personality, born as a male, a Jew, a first-century Palestinian. He was religiously a layman, and as a Jew of his time he was a subject of the Roman Empire. It may seem amazing to twenty-first-century Westerners that Jesus never traveled outside geographical Palestine and the adjoining Decapolis, spoke fluently apparently only one language, wrote nothing that survived him, and did not have the political connections or economic leverage to save himself from a politically expedient trial, unjust condemnation, and execution.

Nevertheless, this very historically particular Jesus was utterly unbounded in his vision of God's design for the human family. Nowhere was this more evident than in his dealings with women, whom he treated not only as equal to men but as his intimate friends and disciples (cf. Jn 11:5; 12:1-8; Lk 8:1-3; 10:38-42). Nothing in Jesus' preaching was meant for men only, and even when a woman implicitly reduced women to their reproductive role, proclaiming blessed the womb and breasts that bore and nurtured Jesus himself, Jesus insisted that women's dignity, like men's, came from hearing and keeping the word of God (Lk 11:27-28). He reversed the discrimination of his disciples who ordered away those, presumably mothers, who brought their children to Jesus for blessing (cf. Lk 18:15-18). Just as he cured a crippled man in the synagogue on the Sabbath (Mk 3:1-6), so he cured a crippled woman in a similar setting, not because she was the possession or dependent of an important man but because she was herself a "daughter of Abraham" (Lk 13:10-17), a member of the covenant in her own right. He raised the daughter of Jairus (Lk 8:40-42, 49-56) as well as the son of the widow of Nain (Lk 7:11-17), recognizing that a girl child is no less precious than a boy, despite society's unequal valuation of them. Jesus accepted the ministry of women to himself (Jn 12:1-7), defended them from the law applied unequally to women (Jn 7:53—8:11), and worked miracles of healing and exorcism for them as for men. To a woman he entrusted the evangelization of the Samaritans, the only preaching ministry of a disciple during Jesus' lifetime in the Gospel of John (Jn 4:28-42). To a woman, his mother, he entrusted the care of those who became his brothers and sisters through his paschal mystery (Jn 19:26). And, most significantly, it was to women he entrusted the Easter proclamation (Mt 28:10; Jn 20:17-18).

The universality of mission that the early Church espoused was rooted in the vision of Jesus himself. God's salvation was not restricted to Jews, to free citizens, to men, or to any other group. It was meant for all people, not to be imposed by the sword or threat of damnation but freely offered by those who themselves had received it without price. We can only marvel that this utterly particular first-century Jewish man somehow transcended the narrowness that had marred religion from long before his birth in the exclusivity of the Jews and has ever since his death and resurrection in the Crusades and persecutions of Christians. Jesus' ultimate allegiance was not to his race, or religion, or gender, or class. It was to the Reign of God, which he discovered in Israel but did not reductively equate with Israel. Somehow Jesus was able to be completely situated in the particularity of one religious tradition but to relativize it by his adherence to the transcendence of God's reign.

Finally, Jesus lived the tension between a *radical subversion of the social, political, and religious status quo and absolute refusal of violence as a means to its demise.* Periodically in the history of New Testament scholarship, the debate reemerges about whether Jesus was or was not a revolutionary. Those who espouse high levels of nondissenting conformity within the Church usually make common cause with those in society who want to carry on the business of this world without interference from the Gospel in maintaining that Jesus was a purely religious figure who eschewed any involvement in the "secular" order. Those committed to social reform in both Church and society and who are convinced that those in power yield it only to force, usually picture Jesus as a kind of rhetorical guerilla urging his followers to overthrow the oppressive Jewish hierarchy and the occupying Roman Empire and return the land and the power to the peasants. In other words, this argument usually has more to do with legitimating current ideologies and agendas than with interpreting Scripture.

104

The picture of Jesus that emerges from the Gospel is much more complex than such dichotomous simplifications suggest. It could be argued that no event in Western history has had the influence on culture that Jesus' brief ministry has exerted. In this sense—that he changed the course of history—Jesus was certainly revolutionary. But it is also virtually undeniable that Jesus did not carry or use weapons, hold office in the religious establishment or in the state, or belong to any of the many revolutionary groups of his time. Furthermore, he did not resist evil when he was arrested, and he died praying for his executioners. Jesus is the model not only of justified revolutionaries but of nonviolent pacifists!

Once again we have to recognize that Jesus' life was a kind of coincidence of opposites, bringing together in his consciousness and his mission approaches to social change that most of his followers continue to dichotomize. Jesus was a religious figure, indeed a mystic, who almost never talked about religion[75] and seems not to have been concerned enough about institutional conformity to insist that his followers observe Sabbath restrictions (cf. Mt 12:1-8) or the ritual aspects of the tradition (cf. Mk 7:1-5). He was casual enough about purity rituals, and free enough even about the Sabbath, to evoke the ire of the local clergy. His preferential teaching form was the parable, and most of his parables were about everyday realities like sheep herding, baking, farming, sewing and weaving, weddings, travel, banquets, housekeeping, stewardship, and wages, subjects that Jesus maintained provided good analogies for talking about the Reign of God. And yet there is no question that the source of Jesus' attraction for his contemporaries was his personal mediation of a God who freely received and accepted everyone, especially "sinners," that is, religious reprobates and social outcasts. Jesus made available a God who cared particularly about those who did not matter in the ecclesiastical and political systems, a God who did not have to be approached with gifts or through officials, who did not have to be placated by ritual observances, who could not be bought and would not be managed. Religion in its true sense, the bond between God and humans, was at the very heart of Jesus' person and message and perhaps that is why he did not have to talk a great deal about it.

Nevertheless, Jesus was so dangerously subversive of the *status quo* in both the religious institution and the sociopolitical establishment that the Jewish hierarchy and the Roman power structure colluded in his execution. He was formally accused of threatening the Temple, which symbolized the whole religious institution, and condemned to death for threatening Roman civil order by occasioning dissent among the people and their leaders and thus civil unrest that could lead to an uprising. In a pattern still often in operation, the state authorities had a vested interest in keeping the collaborating religious hierarchy in control of the people. Jesus, however, told people that they were free and encouraged them to claim that freedom. Jesus announced an alternative reality, a new world in which he encouraged people to take up residence, a social and spiritual order that he called the Reign of God. Nothing is so subversive of dominative regimes as the realization among people that they are free with a God-given freedom that no one, even those who have power to kill the body, can take from them (cf. Mt 10:28). Oppressive regimes need to be certain that there are no available alternatives to the system's arrangements. This is what makes artists and satirists and playwrights more dangerous to oppressive regimes than armed guerillas. Jesus was a free person, a loose cannon in the tightly controlled system, a storyteller who offered alternative visions and invited people to consider another way. It was expedient that this one man be sacrificed (cf. Jn 11:14) before he threatened the "safety," that is, the hopeless submission to the inevitable, of the whole people. Subsequent Christian history has played out over and over again that scenario of Caiphas, the Grand Inquisitor, who knows that people cannot be trusted with freedom and that anyone who stimulates it must be eliminated. Jesus, in short, was both a profoundly religious person who could not be absorbed by the religious institution and a powerfully subversive participant in his society whom no political party or revolutionary agenda could claim.

There is much more to be said about Jesus, but his mediation of these four tensions—between self-gift and self-possession, between belonging to a religious tradition and living a personal spirituality, between historical situation and transcendent focus, between subversion of the *status quo* and nonviolence—is sufficient to reveal the meaning of Christian prophecy. Jesus was a true self, an authentic and self-transcending person who both belonged deeply to history and was neither submerged in it nor merged with it. His identification with God expressed itself in his solidarity with his fellow human beings and made him a powerful voice for the inbreaking of a new world that he called the Reign of God. In this new order it is biblical *shalom*, universal freedom and wholeness for all creation, not particular issues of equality, that controls the agenda. In other words, if we as Christians want to know what justice means and what being the prophetic agents of justice requires, we have our primary resource in the person and message of Jesus.

B. FEMINISM, PROPHECY, AND THE FUTURE

At this point we are positioned to bring together the foregoing considerations about feminism and prophecy to imagine how a prophetic feminist Christianity might contribute to the creation of a future that not only learns from the mistakes of the last century but, more importantly, critically appropriates the gifts and insights that will enable us to generate a new vision based on the person, preaching, and praxis of Jesus. Again, we cannot even survey the whole terrain of possibilities, so I will refocus on the potential of women's Religious Life and particularly its participation in the education of women for prophetic leadership in a new time.

1. Religious Life as a Prophetic Vocation

Religious Life today is, in many important respects, a very different phenomenon from the movement that gave birth to the schools and colleges of the late nineteenth and early twentieth centuries. Perhaps the major difference is that it is no longer a total institution with physically and culturally impermeable boundaries. Religious Life today, like the postconciliar Church of which it is one expression, is deeply integrated into the culture that surrounds and flows through it like the sea through a coral reef. Religious Life is a distinct and specific lifeform in the Church but is no longer isolated, aloof, or alien to the culture of either the rest of the ecclesial body or the postmodern culture emerging in the first world. A major effect of this cultural resituation is that Religious are involved in many enterprises that they neither founded nor control. And in these, as well as endeavors in which they are primary agents, they work closely with colleagues, Catholic and non-Catholic, in enriching mutual interaction. Consequently, whatever I say by way of particular focus about contemporary Religious must be understood in terms of their continual interaction with others who are their equals in faith and commitment, even as they embody that shared faith in different vocations.

Although it has not always been fully faithful to its prophetic call, Religious Life is an essentially prophetic vocation in the Church. In fact, one might say that the combination of the theological and liturgical renewal of the 1940s and '50s, the stimulus of the Council in the '60s, and the emergence of the third wave of feminism in the '70s shook Religious Life out of a long post-Tridentine domestication to the Church's institutional agenda. The reclaiming of its prophetic vocation, and thus of its twofold situation of contemplative immediacy to God and marginality to the social order, is clearly signaled today in the ongoing tension, particularly around involvement in justice issues, between contemporary Religious and some elements of the institutional Church.

The prophetic character of Religious Life as noted above, derives from its self-location in regard to God and to the world. The life is wholly centered on a single-hearted quest for God that excludes all other primary life commitments. This exclusive God-quest gives rise to the lifeform constructed by the vows of consecrated celibacy, evangelical poverty, and obedience, which situates its members, by their own choice, on the margins of their society. As

Thomas Merton reiterated on a number of occasions, the marginal position of Religious Life in relation to the structuring dynamics of society, namely, family life, economic involvement, and political participation, is intrinsic to its prophetic character.[76] It allows Religious to focus in a particular way on the transcendent context of all Christian life, on the critical and transformative role of the Beatitudes in the life of the Church and the world, and thus to help keep in perspective the Church's participation in history which can never be simply identified with secular pursuits, however positive and productive.[77]

This marginal position allows Religious to share, by choice and committed solidarity, the hermeneutical advantage that the poor and oppressed have forced upon them, namely, a view of social systems from the standpoint of those for whom those systems do not work. It is an ambiguous position for Religious precisely because it is chosen and not imposed, but also because it can never be lived absolutely, and thus Religious always experience a kind of "bad faith" or compromised integrity, the unease of the "guilty bystander," in their lofty commitments to unrealizable ideals of single-heartedness, renunciation, and service. But this experienced ambiguity is part of the prophetic vocation and, if allowed to have its purifying and humbling effect, can help prevent complacency or moral arrogance.

Immediacy to God in contemplation and marginalization in society through an evangelical lifestyle position Religious for social criticism, transformative involvement in systemic change, and self-donation to the victims of societal violence and neglect. This prophetic vocation demands the effort to incorporate into one's own life and into that of the Religious community the very tensions Jesus lived as prophet in his own times. Religious are not alone, of course, in struggling to give themselves totally for others without so losing possession of themselves that their ministry degenerates into meaningless activism; to remain faithful to their Catholic Christian tradition, however oppressive it seems at times, without being enticed into collusion with institutional arrogance or exclusivism; to immerse themselves fully in their specific cultural location without losing their transcendent focus; to subvert oppression in both Church and society without succumbing to violence.

Living a prophetic vocation in an ecclesiastical institution that is not only patriarchal but adamantly sexist, especially for women Religious who have internalized a feminist commitment to liberation and justice interpreted through the grid of the Gospel, is a daily and highly stressful challenge. But prophecy is an essentially ecclesial vocation. Religious do not have the option of re-situating their ministry in a secular context so that they can circumvent the problems in the Church. Their vocation, like that of Jeremiah in ancient Israel and Jesus in first-century Judaism, is to live the tensions, to share the burdens of the People of God, even unto death, if that becomes necessary. The purpose of prophecy is to help keep the ecclesial community attuned to and focused on the divine call to fidelity to the covenant in order that it might truly be a light for the nations, drawing all humanity toward God's universal *shalom*.

As I mentioned above, part of living the prophetic vocation is choosing to construct and to live in the kind of community to which we are called by the Gospel. The Religious community, like the Christian family, is meant to be a miniature realization of the right relations, the Gospel ideal of justice, which the Church is called to mediate in this world. The Religious community, being a voluntary society of equal adults who are not bound together by blood, economic necessity, or political power but solely by the love of Jesus can be a striking witness to the meaning of justice, its transcendent source and concrete possibility, and its potential to leaven society with the Gospel.

In short, women's Religious Life today is called to be a corporate integration of the prophetic vocation embodied in Jesus' commitment to justice and the commitment to the full personhood of all people embodied in contemporary feminism. It is a vocation to making and promoting justice, which springs from a contemplative union with God and works itself out in the concrete historical circumstances of Church and world entering a new century.

2. The Education of Women for Prophetic Leadership

Women Religious have virtually always chosen and organized their ministries in function of unmet needs in Church and society. It was the desperate need for education in both faith and the secular disciplines of wave after wave of Catholic immigrants that led to the development in this country, largely by women Religious, of the most extensive religious educational system in world history. As Catholics entered the mainstream of American life and the nation developed a system of universal primary and secondary education, the need for a parallel Catholic system appeared less urgent. The social turmoil of the 1960s, the renewal agenda of Vatican II, the increasing poverty and violence in society at home and abroad, the ravages of the AIDS epidemic, and a number of other developments in the second half of the twentieth century led many Religious congregations to refocus their ministerial energies on needs not being addressed adequately by other agencies.

While some communities, for example, the Holy Cross Sisters, have maintained institutions of higher education for women, like Saint Mary's College, many have seen their colleges closed, transformed into coeducational institutions, or subsumed into more financially viable entities. But even at colleges that have maintained their Catholic and all-women's identity, the student body often includes many non-

Catholics, and the faculty often includes only a small number of Religious working with lay colleagues, both Catholic and non-Catholic. Many of these changes were precipitated by historical forces beyond the control of those affected by them. However, it may be time to reevaluate this situation, taking positive account of the changes of the last thirty years of the twentieth century as we stand on the brink of the twenty-first. It is probably not possible nor desirable to undertake a large-scale refounding of educational institutions of any type, much less those that educate women in a single-sex environment, although the advantages of such an education for many women are indisputable. But we may be in a position to articulate what we learned during the golden age of Catholic higher education for women. Our dreams for a new world order of universal right relations can serve as the launch pad for commitments in our own time that are both continuous with and distinctly different from those of our forebears in the last century. In this final section I want to make some tentative suggestions, not as a program to be undertaken but as an intellectual catalyst for constructive imagining.

First, and vital to any project in this domain, it seems to me that we need to claim, consciously and publicly, without apology or equivocation, our conviction that the feminist vision is not simply one utopian dream among others, the private cause of some disgruntled women, but a crucial factor in the shaping of the future because it is quintessentially a

Gospel vision of full humanity for all persons and right relations among all creatures. Therefore, the women (and men) who embody this feminist vision and commitment have a vital role to play in the present and the future of both Church and society.

In recent years a number of commentators have pointed out that many younger women, especially those in their twenties and thirties, tend to be oblivious of the struggles of their foremothers, which opened educational and economic opportunities for them and their contemporaries. They may regard feminist commitment as passé and assume that the so-called gender wars are over. This is somewhat analogous to the naive and irresponsible assumption that the fall of the Berlin Wall solved the capitalist-communist dilemma and that American-style liberal democracy is the inevitable solution to world problems. If the women who will take the places of those now on the front lines of the struggle for universal ecojustice are to be committed to anything beyond their own immediate well-being in a consumerist enclave of the privileged, they need to be fired by a vision that will not emerge from a standard university program in business administration. The question is, how can the feminist vision and commitment, applied to the issues of a new situation, be transmitted to a generation that can be lulled into false security by the structural changes and the imaginative revisions that predated their experience of adulthood? If the young Catholic women of earlier generations imbibed that vision from the lives as well as the teaching of their protofeminist Religious role models, what is the equivalent resource for women today who are no longer programmed for domesticity but who may well be oblivious of the real obstacles to the feminist agenda of universal justice?

Fortunately, women Religious are no longer virtually alone in the enterprise of the higher education of Catholic women. An impressive corps of religiously committed and spiritually mature professional women scholars and educators are their equal partners in the task. Although it would be impossible to establish scientifically, I would not be surprised if the present generation of women in higher education is not better prepared, personally and academically, than many of their male colleagues simply because breaking into the male-dominated academy has demanded, as one wag put it, that to get half the recognition accorded men, women have to be twice as good. In any case, the role-modeling of life possibilities and social commitment once supplied almost exclusively by women Religious who lived an alternative to traditional female roles is now offered also by laywomen, both married and single. Not only does this provide a more balanced picture of possibilities for women students, but the vital interaction of lay and Religious women scholars and educators, which is so obviously creative for them, can suggest to their students the power of women united across previously impermeable vocational boundaries.

Here I would ask whether women scholars, lay and Religious, have taken full advantage of our common interests and commitments, especially as these can be mobilized for the education and mentoring of younger women? Have we explored the contributions to one another that we could make by a deeper sharing of our lives and commitments from the perspective of our respective vocations?

Second, I would raise the question of whether women educators who have participated in the third wave of feminism, that is, in the broadening and deepening of the feminist agenda from liberal equality of women with men to an ecojustice reconstruction of the social order, have not succumbed in our own way to the apathy we worry about in younger women. Have we assumed that the admission of women, on equal terms, to the institutions of higher education once reserved to men has achieved the objectives of the feminist movement in the educational sphere? Is the participation of women in academic programs created by and for men, the fact that women are qualified to function like men in fields that have not actually modified in any significant way their patriarchal premises or procedures (on the assumption that what is good for men is adequate for women) a resource for the liberation of women and the transformation of society or merely a subtle way of subsuming women into the patriarchal program? But on the other hand, we can legitimately ask whether the concentration of women students committed to the feminist agenda in women's studies programs is actually transforming the educational environment or merely keeping the feminist dynamic safely contained so that it does not subvert the patriarchal structure and agenda of higher education in general. At one time, all-women's colleges offered an alternative model of education. Today most women will be educated in coeducational settings, even if they attend traditionally all-women's institutions. Exhausting as it is, feminist educators need to continue the struggle to transform such institutions from within so that women (and men) students emerge committed to something beyond getting their piece of the economic pie.

Third, one of the most important features of all-women's Catholic colleges was the advanced level of philosophical and theological education they offered their students. By contemporary standards, the preparation of women in the sacred sciences that was typical of women's colleges in the preconciliar period would appear rudimentary, but the recognition that theological learning had to be somehow commensurate with secular learning if women were to exert a strong influence for good in the home or the workplace was fundamental. Today we would frame this conviction in terms of honing the prophetic power of women in the world. If women are to emerge from institutions of higher education committed to the feminist reconstruction of Church

119

and society according to the model of the Gospel's call to liberation and justice, they need not only models of women already engaged in this task and programs of secular studies that embody feminist values, but also the theological and spiritual cultivation that would be the equivalent for today of Sister Madeleva's ideal for women religious educators at midcentury, when she founded the School of Sacred Theology. Have we begun to address, even at Catholic colleges and universities, the question of how best to offer both formal theological education, as distinct from nondenominational religious studies, beyond the secondary level and opportunities for spiritual development beyond basic sacramental services to women students?

The contemporary hunger in this country for spirituality is recognized by many cultural critics, and we know that it is very strong among the young people we have labeled, disrespectfully in my opinion, "generation X." Secular feminism reaches out to younger women through invitations to pro-choice, lesbian, and political activism as well as through professional mentoring. If we want to involve younger Christian women in the world-transforming commitment to faith-inspired feminism, we have to provide opportunities and forums for experiencing that involvement as personally challenging, life-giving, and worth the effort. Religious congregations might reconceive their educational commitment to young women in terms of providing opportunities to participate in the ministries of their congregations and to share life in short- and long-term ways with individual Religious or community groups. Perhaps professional women, lay and Religious, could offer opportunities for retreats and spiritual accompaniment to serious young women in the context of which questions of life commitment and social transformation can be discussed explicitly.

Finally, whether women attend a women's college or a coeducational institution, they will not be taught exclusively by women or by Catholics. Consequently, if we are to be able to hope realistically that all aspects of their postsecondary education will converge toward the formation of intellectually prepared, spiritually mature, and socially committed women, feminist Christian scholars, as colleagues of men and non-Catholics, will have to exert an influence on the educational philosophy, the curriculum, and the programs of the institutions that will not only give women students equal professional and economic opportunities with men, but will actually conduce to their development as women and as feminists. How do we help men, especially men of good will who really want to foster the development of their women students and who share the Gospel commitment to the transformation of society, become feminists? What concrete effect on our curricula does feminist Christian commitment have? Do all classes, no matter who teaches them, take adequate account of the feminist critique, feminist resources, and feminist method?

All of the questions raised in this section presuppose that there is no longer any question about whether feminism should be actively promoted among our students, especially but not exclusively our women students. If feminism is defined as an intellectual, spiritual, and practical commitment to the full personhood of every human being and right relationships among all creatures, it must be espoused by Christians as a Gospel imperative. The times have changed, and the circumstances in which the education of women takes place have changed. Our understanding of feminism has changed, as has our understanding of the relationship between the Church and the world. But the gospel call to prophetic engagement in the transformation of the world into the Reign of God has not changed, nor has the model of that vocation, who is Christ, yesterday, today, and the same forever.

CONCLUSION

The sheer speed of life, the glut of fragmented information with which technology inundates us, the enormity of human crises all over the world and the immediacy with which they are forced upon our consciousness by the media, the vastness and unmanageability of the material universe crashing in upon us conspire to make constructive engagement with the twenty-first century seem totally beyond our capacities. The temptation to resign from the project, to build a cocoon in which to enjoy what we can as long as we last, can be overwhelming. How do we sustain Christian hope, marshal renewed energy to stay the course as disciples of Jesus Christ committed to a future in which right relations among all beings and first of all among humans will be achieved? Our situation seems immensely more confused and complicated than that of any generation of Christians that preceded us.

But there is a story in the Gospel that suggests that every generation faces this temptation to drop out, to despair of a too distant ideal, and to abandon responsibility for a future one may not live to see. It is the story in Matthew 25:1–13 of the ten virgins awaiting the return of the bridegroom, an eschatological parable about the coming of Christ at the end of time. The bridegroom is long delayed in the historical task of the salvation of the world, and his servants, the ten virgins, grow weary in their waiting. But despite their fatigue, five of them were wise enough to have filled their lamps with oil, a biblical metaphor for eschatological preparedness, which only makes sense to those whose faith and hope are undaunted. Somehow they knew, they insisted on hoping, that however long the delay the bridegroom would finally come. Perhaps we are meant to realize that not filling their lamps, not doing the little that they could do, was an implicit surrender by the other five to despair of Christ's project. Why prepare for what looks impossible and will probably never happen? But despair, in gospel terms, is not adult realism; it is ultimate folly. Christ alone is the Savior of the world. It is, in the end, his work, not ours. But we human beings (how appropriately symbolized by faithful women!) can be steadfast in hope, doing what little lies in our power to cooperate with that great work. Only the truly wise, those who are spiritually virginal in their single-minded commitment to the bridegroom and who espouse unshaken hope in his ultimate victory, can find the energy, muster the inventiveness, make the necessary effort, and wake up in time to meet the Savior of the world with lamps trimmed. The light of truth shining in the darkness is borne by those who are ready, with oil in their lamps.

Notes

1. I am indebted for my acquaintance with Madeleva's life and work to Gail Porter Mandell, *Madeleva: A Biography* (Albany, N.Y.: State University of New York Press, 1997). I also wish to thank my research assistant, Jan Richardson, for her invaluable assistance in preparing this manuscript.
2. I offered this definition and elaborated on each member of it in *Beyond Patching: Faith and Feminism in the Catholic Church,* The 1990 Anthony Jordan Lectures at Newman Theolog-ical College, Edmonton (New York/Mahwah, N.J.: Paulist Press, 1991), 15-31.
3. Virginia Woolf wrote in *A Room of One's Own* (New York: Harcourt Brace & World, 1929), 4, "...a woman must have money and a room of her own if she is to write...."
4. See Margaret Gill Hein, "Attendance Policy," in *The Encyclopedia of Educational Research*, 5th ed., vol. 1 (New York: Free Press, 1982), 174.
5. See Julia Wrigley, "Gender and Education in the Welfare State," in *Education and Gender Equality*, edited by Julia Wrigley (Bristol, Pa.: Falmer Press, 1992), 1-23.

6. See J. Brophy, "Interaction of Male and Female Students with Male and Female Teachers," in *Gender Influences in Classroom Interaction*, edited by Louise Cherry Wilkinson and Cora Bagley Marrett (Orlando: Academic Press, 1985); Donna Eder, "Ability Grouping as Self-Fulfilling Prophecy: A Micro-Analysis of Teacher-Student Interaction," *Sociology of Education* 54 (July, 1981): 151-62.

7. See Wrigley, "Gender and Education," 15-16.

8. See Walter J. Ong, *Fighting for Life: Contest, Sexuality, and Consciousness* (Ithaca, N.Y.: Cornell University Press, 1981), for a penetrating analysis of the influence on education of male self-definition in terms of competition. See Mary Field Belenky, Blythe McVicker Clinchy, Nancy Rule Goldberger, and Jill Mattuck Tarule, *Women's Ways of Knowing: The Development of Self, Voice, and Mind* (New York: Basic Books, 1986), for a well-researched discussion of how women, in contrast to men, learn.

9. For discussion and further resources on women's representation in various professional fields, see Jerry A. Jacobs, "The Sex Segregation of Occupations: Structural Approaches," in *Women and Work: A Handbook*, edited by Paula J. Dubeck and Kathryn Borman (New York: Garland, 1996), 114-16; Rodolfo Alvarez, et al., "Women in the Professions: Assessing Progress," in Dubeck and Borman, 118-23. Section 3 of

this volume, entitled "Women in Diverse Occupations" (139-226), includes a variety of short articles dealing with women in science, journalism, broadcasting, law, public accounting, the military, factory work, and so on.

10. An article by Linda Grant and Kathryn B. Ward, "Women in Academia," in Dubeck and Borman, 165-67, cogently summarizes recent statistical research in this area, documenting many instances in which women faculty continue to encounter a "glass ceiling" in regard to advances in salary, promotion and tenure, and access to policy-making positions in institutions of higher learning. In "Women of Color in Academe," Mia Tuan, et al. (in Dubeck and Borman, 168-73), focus on the combination of gender and race in the functioning of discrimination within the academy.

11. For a discussion of the economic situation of women throughout this century, see Claudia Goldin, *Understanding the Gender Gap: An Economic History of American Women* (New York/Oxford: Oxford University Press, 1990). On page 212 she notes that due to the rising divorce rate over the past several decades, there has been a related rise in paternal default, so "more women are raising children on their income alone. A mother's income, moreover, is likely to be less than a father's because of her lower past investments in marketable skills....As a result,...considerably more women than men are in poverty."

12. The Educational Act passed by Congress in 1972 included a section, Title IX, which stated, "No person in the United States shall, on the basis of sex, be excluded from participation in, be denied the benefits of, or be subjected to discrimination under any educational programs or activities receiving federal financial assistance." Susan K. Cahn, *Coming On Strong: Gender and Sexuality in Twentieth-Century Women's Sport* (New York: Macmillan, 1994), 250, states that this was the first time that a woman's right to equal treatment in high school and college athletics was codified in law and that it ushered in a revolution in women's participation in sports. See also David F. Salter, *Crashing the Old Boys' Network: The Tragedies and Triumphs of Girls and Women in Sports* (Westport, Conn.: Praeger, 1996), 55-66, for a thorough discussion of the problems the courts have had in enforcing Title IX in the twenty-five years since its passage.

13. See *Sport*, edited by John Coleman and Gregory Baum, *Concilium* 205 (Edinburgh, Scotland: T. & T. Clark, 1989).

14. Joyner won three gold medals at the 1988 Summer Olympics in Seoul, Korea (Cahn, *Coming On Strong*, 252).

15. See the history of the School of Sacred Theology in Mandell, *Madeleva*, 183-91.

16. Paula D. Nesbitt notes that in 1992, women made up 30 percent of the student body in U.S. and

Canadian seminaries overall and up to 50 percent or more in moderate to liberal seminaries, with similar increases in the schools of Jewish traditions that ordain women ("Women Clergy," in Dubeck and Borman, 181–84). That trend has continued since 1992 and seems likely to increase rather than decrease.

17. At this writing a woman is president of the CTS and the AAR, and women have headed the CBA, the CTSA, and CLSA in the past two years.

18. All of the Madeleva Lectures have been published by Paulist Press.

19. Elisabeth Schüssler Fiorenza, *In Memory of Her: A Feminist Theological Reconstruction of Christian Origins* (New York: Crossroad, 1985).

20. Catherine Mowry LaCugna, *God for Us: The Trinity and Christian Life* (San Francisco: Harper, 1991); Elizabeth A. Johnson, *She Who Is: The Mystery of God in Feminist Theological Discourse* (New York: Crossroad, 1992).

21. Rosemary Radford Ruether, "Christology and Feminism: Can a Male Saviour Save Women?" in *To Change the World: Christology and Cultural Criticism* (New York: Crossroad, 1981), 45–56, originally given as part of the Kuyper Lectures at the Free University in Amsterdam in September 1980.

22. See chapter V, paragraphs 25–33 of *Inter Insigniores* (Declaration on the Admission of Women to the Ministerial Priesthood) of the Sacred Congregation for the Doctrine of the Faith,

1976, available in English in Austin P. Flannery, ed., *Vatican Council II: The Conciliar and Postconciliar Documents*, vol. 2 (Grand Rapids: Eerdmans, 1984), 338–42.

23. See, e.g., Ruether, *To Change the World;* Mary C. Boys, *Jewish-Christian Dialogue: One Woman's Experience*, 1997 Madeleva Lecture in Spirituality (New York/Mahwah, N.J.: Paulist Press, 1997).

24. The recent warning about Anthony De Mello's work in East-West spirituality, the ongoing investigation of the work of Jacques Dupuis, especially his *Toward a Christian Theology of Religious Pluralism* (Maryknoll, N.Y.: Orbis, 1997), and the tension around the understanding of evangelization evidenced in the Asian Synod of Bishops testify to the the anxiety of the Vatican over the question of the uniqueness of Jesus. For a good, brief overview of the state of the question, see the article by John L. Allen, Jr.: "Doubts about Dialogue," in *National Catholic Reporter* 35, no. 37 (August 27, 1999): 14–16.

25. Joan Chittister, *Job's Daughters: Women and Power,* 1990 Madeleva Lecture in Spirituality (New York/Mahwah, N.J.: Paulist Press, 1990).

26. Denise Lardner Carmody, *An Ideal Church: A Meditation,* 1999 Madeleva Lecture in Spirituality (New York/Mahwah, N.J.: Paulist Press, 1999).

27. Mary Collins, *Women at Prayer,* 1987 Madeleva Lecture in Spirituality (New York/Mahwah, N.J.: Paulist Press, 1987).

28. Lisa Sowle Cahill, *Women and Sexuality,*1992 Madeleva Lecture in Spirituality (New York/Mahwah, N.J.: Paulist Press, 1992).

29. Margaret A. Farley, *Personal Commitments: Beginning, Keeping, Changing* (San Francisco: Harper & Row, 1986).

30. Even such a measured and restrained commentator as the late Cardinal Basil Hume, in his final lecture delivered posthumously by Archbishop Oscar Lipscomb, called attention to the problem. See *One in Christ: Unity and Diversity in the Church Today* (New York: National Pastoral Life Center, 1999), esp. p. 11.

31. Carol Gilligan, *In a Different Voice: Psychological Theory and Women's Development* (Cambridge, Mass.: Harvard University Press, 1982).

32. For a good discussion of this topic, see Brian V. Johnstone, "From Physicalism to Personalism," *Studia Moralia* 30 (1992): 71–96. See also Margaret A. Farley, *Just Love: Sexual Ethics and Social Change* (New York: Continuum, 1997).

33. E.g., John Gray, *Men Are from Mars, Women Are from Venus: A Practical Guide for Improving Communication and Getting What You Want in Your Relationships* (New York: HarperCollins, 1992).

34. See James Gleick, *Chaos: Making a New Science* (New York: Penguin, 1987), 83–118, for the fascinating story of Mandelbrot's peregrinations among the sciences, theoretical and applied, and the amazing results.

35. Rosemary Radford Ruether, *Sexism and God-Talk* (Boston: Beacon Press, 1993).

36. Catherine Mowry LaCugna, ed., *Freeing Theology: The Essentials of Theology in Feminist Perspective* (San Francisco: Harper, 1993).

37. Belenky, et al., *Women's Ways of Knowing;* see note 8 above for full reference.

38. A standard treatment of interdisciplinarity as the emerging shape of much contemporary scholarship is Julie Thompson Klein, *Interdisciplinarity: History, Theory, and Practice* (Detroit: Wayne State University Press, 1990).

39. For a clear statement of this in relation to biblical studies see A. K. M. Adam, *What Is Postmodern Biblical Criticism?* (Minneapolis: Fortress, 1995), 62.

40. See Sandra M. Schneiders, "Feminist Spirituality," in *The New Dictionary of Catholic Spirituality,* edited by Michael Downey (Collegeville, Minn.: Liturgical Press, 1993), 394–406, for a fuller exploration of this aspect of feminism.

41. See Christine Downing, *The Goddess: Mythological Images of the Feminine* (New York: Crossroad, 1981); Carol P. Christ, *Womenspirit Rising: A Feminist Reader in Religion* (San Francisco: Harper & Row, 1979). Both of these authors have continued to write in the area of spirituality and the study of religion from a feminist perspective.

42. Mary Daly, *Beyond God the Father: Toward a Philosophy of Women's Liberation* (Boston, Beacon

Press, 1985; orig. 1973). Rosemary Radford Ruether also began publishing on sexism in the Church in the 1970s, e.g., *Religion and Sexism: Images of Women in the Jewish and Christian Traditions*, edited by Rosemary Radford Ruether (New York: Simon & Schuster, 1974); *New Woman, New Earth: Sexist Ideologies and Human Liberation* (New York: Seabury, 1975). Both Daly and Ruether have produced steady streams of feminist writing since their publications in the early 1970s. Daly has become explicitly post-Christian while Ruether remains a strong but loyal voice of protest within Catholicism.

43. The Women's Ordination Conference was founded in 1975 in Detroit, Michigan. See *Women and Catholic Priesthood: An Expanded Vision*, Proceedings of the Detroit Ordination Conference, edited by Anne Marie Gardiner (New York/Mahwah, N.J.: Paulist Press, 1976), for a full report of the conference, which called for the establishment of WOC.

44. After *Inter Insigniores* (1976), John Paul II issued an apostolic letter, *Ordinatio Sacerdotalis* (1995), in which he reiterated the position that the Church has no authority to ordain women. The Sacred Congregation for the Doctrine of the Faith issued a *responsum* to the question of whether the teaching presented in the pope's letter "belongs to the deposit of faith" (1995), saying that it did and therefore required the definitive assent of the faith-

ful. Finally, Cardinal Ratzinger issued a commentary on John Paul II's *motu proprio, Tuendam Fidem* (1998), in which Ratzinger gives as an example of truths that must be held without dissent or question, "the doctrine that priestly ordination is reserved only to men." For a careful appraisal of the *responsum* by the Catholic Theological Society of America, see "Appendix A: Tradition and the Ordination of Women," edited by Judith A. Dwyer, *CTSA Proceedings* 54 (1997): 197–204.

45. To date, Priests for Equality has published the *Inclusive Responsorial Psalms, Cycle C* and *Cycle A* (West Hyattsville, Md.: Priests for Equality, 1990/1992), as well as the *Inclusive Lectionary Texts, Cycle C* and *Cycle A* (1992/1994), the *Inclusive New Testament* (1994), and *The Inclusive Psalms* (1997). Also, the Catholic Biblical Association has been seeking approval for an inclusive-language version of the Bible and of liturgical texts since the early 1990s. For a detailed history of these efforts from 1990 through 1997, as well as the text of the statement by the National Conference of Catholic Bishops of November 15, 1990, entitled *Criteria for the Evaluation of Inclusive Language Translations of Scriptural Texts Proposed for Liturgical Use*," see the web site at: http://students.cua.edu/org/cbib/watch.htm . For an up-to-date summary of the situation, see Ronald D. Witherup, "Inclusive Language: An Issue Revisited," *Priest* 55 (August, 1999): 30–37.

46. See Ronald D. Witherup, *A Liturgist's Guide to Inclusive Language* (Collegeville, Minn.: Liturgical Press, 1996), which argues that the failure of Church officials to heed the desire of the majority of Catholics for inclusive language in the liturgy is leading to a much worse alternative in the form of "wildcat" language changing by people who are not equipped to do so. Thomas H. Groome, *Language for a "Catholic" Church* (Kansas City, Mo.: Sheed & Ward, 1991), offers a very good, pastorally sensitive argument for the use of inclusive language in liturgy and a practical program for helping people learn to use such language.

47. *Catechism of the Catholic Church* (Collegeville, Minn.: Liturgical Press, 1994).

48. *Humanae Vitae* (Encyclical Letter on the Regulation of Births) available in Flannery, vol. 2, 397–416.

49. For an explanation of the theological category "reception," see Thomas P. Rausch, "Reception," in *The New Dictionary of Theology*, edited by Joseph A. Komonchak, Mary Collins, and Dermot A. Lane (Wilmington, Del.: Michael Glazier, 1987), 828-30.

50. For a discussion of the response to *Humanae Vitae* since its publication, including statistical data on the practice of contraception among Catholic women, see Megan Hartman, "*Humanae Vitae*: Thirty Years of Discord and Dissent," *Conscience* 19, no. 3 (Autumn, 1998): 8-16.

51. For the official position see *Quaestio de abortu*, promulgated in 1974 and available in English translation as "Declaration on Procured Abortion" in Flannery, vol. 2, 441–53.

52. For comparative statistics on abortion attitudes among mainline Christians and non-Christians, see *Christianity Today* 41 (April 28, 1997): 84. For an analysis of the surveys commissioned by Americans United for Life and by the National Conference of Catholic Bishops in 1989, see James R. Kelly, "Abortion: What Americans *Really* Think and the Catholic Challenge," *America* 165 (November 2, 1991): 310–16.

53. Although to a large extent this scenario is hypothetical since the vast majority of cases involving the life of the mother can be resolved through application of the principle of double effect, which involves indirect abortion, the principle many feminists would defend is that the life of a woman is at least as valuable as that of a fetus and to the woman concerned may legitimately have the superior claim.

54. A valuable resource on the identity, numbers, distribution, and institutions of U.S. women Religious is George C. Stewart, *Marvels of Charity: History of American Sisters and Nuns*, Foreword by Dolores Liptak (Huntington, Ind.: Our Sunday Visitor, 1994).

55. The History of Women Religious Network, coordinated by Karen Kennelly, was formed in 1987

and is dedicated to the promotion of research and publication on the subject.

56. See the Augsburg Confession, 27. English translation is available as *The Augsburg Confession: A Confession of Faith Presented in Augsburg by Certain Princes and Cities to His Imperial Majesty Charles V in the Year 1530* (Philadelphia: Fortress Press, 1980). Luther's theological rejection of monasticism led to the expunging of Religious Life from mainstream Protestantism and Anglicanism followed suit.

57. See Patricia Wittberg, *Pathways to Re-Creating Religious Communities* (New York/Mahwah, N.J.: Paulist Press, 1996), 19–31, where she explains the sociological category of the "religious virtuoso" and applies it to women Religious.

58. I dealt with this topic in "Religious Life: The Dialectic Between Marginality and Transformation," *Spirituality Today* 40 (Winter 1988, supplement): 59–79, and take it up in greater detail in *Religious Life in a New Millennium*, vol. 1, *Finding the Treasure: Locating Catholic Religious Life in a New Ecclesial and Cultural Context* (New York/Mahwah, N.J.: Paulist Press, 2000).

59. This egalitarianism was seriously eroded in men's orders when some of the monks were ordained and thus came to be seen, whatever their position in the community, as ontologically superior to nonordained members. The problem this has caused in men's orders is discussed from

a number of vantage points *in A Concert of Charisms: Ordained Ministry in Religious Life*, edited by Paul K. Hennessy (New York/Mahwah, N.J.: Paulist Press, 1997).

60. A good discussion of this pioneer function of Religious Life can be found in Catherine M. Harmer, *Religious Life in the 21st Century: A Contemporary Journey into Canaan* (Mystic, Conn.: Twenty-Third Publications, 1995), esp. 79–82.

61. In 1965, for example, according to the statistics collected by Stewart, *Marvels of Charity*, 449, there were 4,566,809 pupils in Catholic parochial schools and 1,095,519 students in Catholic high schools. The vast majority of these were taught by women Religious.

62. In the 1940s Sister Catherine Bertrand, D.C., did a study of the education of women Religious, which was published *as The Education of Sisters: A Plan for Integrating the Religious, Cultural, Social, and Professional Training of Sisters* (New York: Sheed & Ward, 1941) and which documented the serious lack of professional preparation of Sisters and the need to remedy that lack. Her work helped prepare the way for the founding of the Sister Formation Movement a few years later. By the mid-1960s the requirement that all Sisters be professionally prepared for the work they would do was fairly well accepted not only by Religious superiors but by the hierarchy that had originally opposed higher education for Sisters.

63. The LCWR was originally called the Conference of Major Superiors of Women (CMSW) and grew out of the Institutes on Spirituality, which began meeting at Notre Dame University in 1952. The CMSW was inaugurated in 1956 and was officially approved by the Vatican in 1962. Its first president was an Adrian Dominican, Mother Gerald Barry. This move toward organizing across congregational lines was instigated by Pope Pius XII, who began encouraging renewal of women's congregations as early as 1950.

64. Cynthia Russett and Tracy Schier, eds., *Beyond the Seven Sisters: Historical Perspectives on Colleges Founded by Women Religious.* The project is situated in the history department of Yale University, and the editors expect publication sometime in 2000. My thanks to Jeanne Knoerle for alerting me to this work and to Tracy Schier for sharing some of the manuscript with me prior to its publication.

65. Barbara Johns, I.H.M., "In Their Own Image: Shaping Women's Education at Detroit's Immaculata High School," *Building Sisterhood: A Feminist History of the Sisters, Servants of the Immaculate Heart of Mary*, edited by Margaret Susan Thompson (Syracuse, N.Y.: Syracuse University Press, 1997), 320–53.

66. Johns, "In Their Own Image," 352.

67. Charlotte Perkins Gilman wrote her delightful utopian novel, *Herland* (New York: Pantheon, 1979) in 1915 to exalt a vision of women as free, autonomous, and self-sufficient but eminently social and responsible subjects of their own lives. The women lived in an all-woman society in an enclave in the mountains discovered by three men through whom Gilman hilariously satirizes the male of the species as underdeveloped humans unable to comprehend a peaceful, cooperative, and productive world, especially one in which men played no role at all, much less that of leadership.

68. A survey of 894 women involved in Catholic ministry concluded on March 16, 1999, and analyzed and reported by Maureen Fiedler, Karen Schwarz, and Andrea Johnson of the Women's Ordination Conference in *New Women, New Church* 22 (Fall, 1999): 1, 3, found that of the 265 respondents who claimed to experience a call to ordained ministry 54 percent said that the Church is too patriarchal for women to seek ordination at this time.

69. See, e.g., a version of the Bem Androgyny Scale, which can be found in Carol Tavris and Carole Wade, *The Longest War: Sex Differences in Perspective*, 2nd ed. (Orlando, Fla.: Harcourt Brace Jovanovich, 1984).

70. See Joann Wolski Conn, "Dancing in the Dark: Women's Spirituality and Ministry," in *Women's*

Spirituality: Resources for Christian Development, edited by Joann Wolski Conn, 2nd ed. (New York/Mahwah, N.J.: Paulist Press, 1996), 29; see also in this volume, Jean Baker Miller, "The Development of Women's Sense of Self," 165-84.

71. The so-called "butterfly effect," or sensitive dependence on initial conditions, is described in Gleick, *Chaos*, 20-23.

72. I found Kathryn Tanner's *Theories of Culture: A New Agenda for Theology* (Minneapolis: Fortress Press, 1997) very stimulating on this point.

73. A good introduction to contemporary theory about biblical prophecy is Thomas Overholt, *Channels of Prophecy: The Social Dynamics of Prophetic Activity* (Minneapolis: Fortress Press, 1989).

74. An engaging presentation of Jesus as prophet rooted in a profound experience of God is Marcus J. Borg's *Jesus, A New Vision: Spirit, Culture, and the Life of Discipleship* (San Francisco: Harper & Row, 1987) and *Meeting Jesus Again For the First Time: The Historical Jesus and the Heart of Contemporary Faith* (San Francisco: Harper & Row, 1994).

75. Amos Niven Wilder, *Early Christian Rhetoric: The Language of the Gospel* (Cambridge: Harvard University Press, 1964), esp. ch. 1, pp. 1-17, made this obvious but startling observation, pointing to the secular character of Jesus' parables as a major factor in their accessibility and appeal.

76. Thomas Merton returned frequently to this topic but dealt with it most extensively in *A Vow of Conversation: Journals, 1964-1965*, edited by and with a preface by Naomi Burton Stone (New York: Farrar, Straus, Giroux, 1988).
77. This prophetic role of Religious Life was recognized by the Council in *Lumen Gentium*, VI, 44. English translation is available in Austin P. Flannery, ed. *Documents of Vatican II*, vol. 1, rev. ed. (Grand Rapids: Eerdmans, 1988 [orig., 1975]), 350-423.

The Madeleva Lecture in Spirituality

This series, sponsored by the Center for Spirituality, Saint Mary's College, Notre Dame, Indiana, honors annually the woman who as president of the college inaugurated its pioneering graduate program in theology, Sister M. Madeleva, C.S.C.

1985
Monika K. Hellwig
Christian Women in a Troubled World

1986
Sandra M. Schneiders
Women and the Word

1987
Mary Collins
Women at Prayer

1988
Maria Harris
Women and Teaching

1989
Elizabeth Dreyer
Passionate Women: Two Medieval Mystics

1990
Joan Chittister, O.S.B.
Job's Daughters

1991
Dolores R. Leckey
Women and Creativity

1992
Lisa Sowle Cahill
Women and Sexuality

1993
Elizabeth A. Johnson
Women, Earth, and Creator Spirit

1994
Gail Porter Mandell
Madeleva: One Woman's Life

1995
Diana L. Hayes
Hagar's Daughters

1996
Jeanette Rodriguez
Stories We Live
Cuentos Que Vivimos

1997
Mary C. Boys
Jewish-Christian Dialogue

1998
Kathleen Norris
The Quotidian Mysteries

1999
Denise Lardner Carmody
An Ideal Church: A Meditation